BOO(
COCKT......

"Make your party special"

200 Cocktails

This book contains a selection of cocktail recipes to make your parties unforgettable in 2021.

The drinks presented are made with different ingredients and combinations from the usual cocktails to have something original for your friends or relatives to taste.

COCKTAILS LIST

Pornostar Martini, Tsunami, No Stress, Spirit of the Union, Gummy Bear, Amarula Magic, Blue Lagoon, Butterfly, Oyster Bloody Mary, Surfer On Acid, Red Headed, Sunset Solero, French Martini, Night of Rose, Mint Julep, Grinch, Gimlet, Salty Dog, Raspberry Mojito, Accomplice, Gin Rickey, Ramos Gin Fizz, Caipirinha, Cheeky Vimto, Singapore Sling, Alaska, White Russian, Espresso Martini, Tequila Sunrise, Dark Stormy, Negroni, John Collins, El Diablo, Clover Club, B52, Volcano,Screwdriver, Pain Killer, WooWoo, Bucks Fizz, El Presidente, Rum Runner, Maitai, Black Russian, Black Stripe, Bloody Margaret, Blushing Bride, Bramble, Air Attack, Fallen Angel, Kingston, Kiss on the Lips, Kaalis Envy, Kahlua Mint Slide, Whipped Iced Milk, Upside Down Hypnotic..........

.........AND MANY MANY OTHER........
.........DELICIOUS RECIPES.........

PORNSTAR MARTINI

Adapted from a drink created in 2002 by Douglas Ankrah at The Townhouse bar in Knightsbridge, London. Douglas also founded London's LAB bar which is also often associated with this drink.

Ingredients
1½ fresh Passionfruit (fresh fruit)
60 ml Ketel One Vodka (infused with vanilla)
15 ml Passoa 'The Passion Drink' Liqueur
15 ml Le Sirop de Monin Vanilla Sugar Syrup (Vanille)
15 ml Freshly squeezed lime juice
60 ml Brut Champagne

How To make a Porn Star Martini
To make a great tasting Porn Star Martini you'll need to flavour your vodka with a vanilla pod. Simply cut the vanilla pod lengthways to expose the flavoursome seeds inside and drop the scored vanilla pod into your bottle of vodka. Reseal and shake the

bottle several times a day for at least two days, preferably a week.

To make your cocktail, wash and cut 2 fresh passion fruits in half, Scoop out the seeds and flesh of 3 halves into your shaker. (Keep the last passion fruit half for garnish). Add the next four ingredients (all but champagne), Shake with ice and fine strain into chilled glass.

Separately, Pour champagne into a chilled shot glass to serve on the side. Instruct drinker to sip alternately from each glass.

TSUNAMI

Ingredients

1 o.z red sambuca and tequila

½ o.z blue curacao

½ o.z triple sec vodka

½ o.z malibu

½ o.z gin

How To make a The Tsunami

Put ice till top in a long glass.

Add sambuca and tequila.

In a shaker add ice blue curacao triple sec vodka malibu and gin shake well
Then open the shaker, add some lemonade and then stir it.
Pour it slowly in the glass till top.

NO STRESS

Ingredients

1 o.z Coconut cream
1 o.z Pineapple juice
1 o.z rum

How To make a No Stress

Shake all in a shaker with ice
Put it in a martini glass
And then pour the blue curaçao slowly till half the glass.
At the end pour one o.z of strawberry or watermelon syrup slowly.

SPIRIT OF THE UNION

A cocktail created to pay tribute for the UAE community and true art of whisky blending.

Ingredients
60ML Chivas Regal 12,
25ML Crisp pear and Date syrup,
25ML Clarified Lemon Juice,
15ML Pear Puree,
2Dashes Peychaud's Bitters ,
2Dashes Plum Bitters.

Garnish: Color of UAE flag

SWITCHEL

Ingredients
1 1/2 oz. Gin or vodka
1 oz DRAM Ginger Switchel
2 oz sparkling water
 cinnamon
any flavor DRAM Bitters - this drink works with all of them.

How To make a Switchel

In a cocktail glass muddle Rosemary, add booze, switchel, cinnamon and ice and shake well. Strain over fresh ice and top with sparkling water and your favorite flavor DRAM bitters.

This refreshing cocktail uses a bit of Switchel which is a blend of apple cider vinegar and pure honey that was traditionally enjoyed by farmers to keep them hydrated and nourished throughout the day. Our new Ginger flavor lends itself well to almost all kinds of liquor and we particularly love it with a nice clean gin or vodka. This drink may also be enjoyed sans booze and is just as satisfying.

GUMMY BEAR

Ingredients

1/2 ounce Amaretto
1/2 ounce grenadine
1/2 ounce melon liqueur (Midori)
3 ounces orange juice
3 ounces pineapple juice
1/2 ounce Southern Comfort

How To make a Gummy Bear
Mix all the ingredients in a shaker with ice.
Pour in a tall glass filled with ice.
You can put a splash of 7-up.
This pretty little cocktail tastes just like fruit
punch. I used fresh and squeezed orange juice
and feel happy that I am getting 89% of my
vitamin c for the day!

AMARULA MAGIC COCKTAIL

Ingredients
25ml Amarula Cream
25ml Peppermint Liqueur
25ml Kahlua
Sprig of mint for

How To make a Amarula Magic
Mix together in a cocktail shaker with some
ice.
Strain into a tumbler over ice-cubes.

Garnish with fresh mint.

A delicious, sweet and minty aperitif that has a surprisingly refreshing nature. Enjoyed slowly as a sundowner, it produces magic as night falls!

BLUE LAGOON

Ingredients
50 ml White Mischief Vodka
200 ml Blue Curacao
100 ml Lemonade
1 orange slice
Ice cubes

How To make a Blue Lagoon
In a cocktail shaker, combine all the ingredients in the defined quantity along with some ice cubes.
Give it a nice shake and serve it in a Highball Glass or a Martini Glass.

Garnish the brim with an orange slice.

BUTTERFLY

Ingredients
1oz Malibu Rum
1oz Blue Curacao
1oz Cherry Vodka
Sprite
Ice
Black sanding sugar
Simple syrup

How To make a Hookah Butterfly
Decorating the rim of your glassware
Get 2 appetizer plates on one of them out
about 1 tbsp (tablespoon) of simple syrup. On
the other one add sanding sugar.
Dip the rim of your glasses in the simple syrup
and then in the sanding sugar set to the side
Fill your glassware with ice only 3/4 of the
way full
Pour the liquors in order as listed above into
the glass
Top with sprite
Lightly stir.

OYSTER BAR BLOODY MARY

Ingredients
1 bottle of vodka
2 to 3 large cans of tomato juice (46-oz. cans)
20-oz. bottle of Worcestershire sauce
10-oz. bottle of Tabasco
2 tbsp. salt
1 tbs. black pepper
1 pint white vinegar
Celery stalk
Horseradish
Juice of two lemons
Juice of two limes

How To make a Oyster Bar Bloody Mary
The night before your tailgate party:
Add all ingredients, except the vodka and horseradish in a gallon container.
Store and refrigerate.
At the tailgate party:
Fill each tailgater's cup with ice.
Pour 1-1/2 oz. of vodka over ice.
Add a dollop of horseradish.
Top with Bloody Mary mix.

Stir with celery stalk and serve with a smile.

SURFER ON ACID

Ingredients
25 ml Coconut Rum,
25 ml Jagermeister,
25 ml Pineapple Juice

How To make a Surfer On Acid
Pour the ingredients into a cocktail shaker
filled with ice. Shake well. Strain into a chilled
cocktail glass.

If you find the flavour of the mighty
Jagermeister spirit a little "imposing", then
this cocktail could be for you, as the coconut
and Pineapple work together to create a mild
and tasty mix.

RED HEADED

Ingredients
50 ml Jagermeister,
50 ml Peach Schnapps, Cranberry Juice

How To make a RedHeaded

Combine Jägermeister and schnapps in glass full of ice. Add cranberry juice to fill to top. Stir as necessary and serve iced cold.

A particularly popular in America, the RedheadedSlut has a very unique taste, which is actually surprisingly good. The drink gets its name from the cranberry juice that separates itself from the rest of the drink. The Redheaded Slut is also popular as a shooter, in which you can reduce the measurements to 5 ounces peach schnapps, 10 ounces Jagermeister and 15 ounces cranberry juice, shaken in a cocktail shaker with ice and poured in a shot glass.

The Redheaded slut is also known as the Ginger Bitch and it was apparently first created at O'Grady's Pub in Ohio in 2000. The Drink became very popular at bars among college-aged adults, who were intrigued by the sexual name of the drink. There are a few variations on this drink, such as the Lindsey Lohan cocktail plus a popular variation with the same name that uses equal parts Jagermeister, Crown Royal, Southern Comfort and cranberry-flavoured vodka. This version is a much more potent drink and is not for the faint-hearted.

The Redheaded Slut is one of the easier drinking cocktails which include the intensely flavoured Jagermesiter, which is a German proof digestif made with herbs and spices and is typically 35% ABV. The cranberry juice and peach schnapps bring a sweet fruit flavour to the herbal tasting Jagermeister and this helps balance the drink and make it very quaffable.

SUNSET SOLERO

Ingredients
30 ml Spiced Rum
15 ml Passoa
15 ml Galliano Vanilla
30 ml Passion Fruit Coulis
30 ml Orange Juice
30 ml Pineapple Juice
1/4 of a fresh Lime
A splash of Grenadine
Slices of fresh Peach

Preparation

It is an amazing drink! Our Sunset Solero Cocktail is made with Spiced Rum, Galliano Vanilla, Passion Fruit Coulis, Orange Juice, Pineapple Juice, Lime, Grenadine, and Peach slices!

Garnish with slices of fresh Peach

FRENCH MARTINI

Ingredients

25 ml Vodka

25 ml Chambord

75 ml Pineapple Juice

3 Raspberries for Garnish

Preparation

Pour the ingredients into a cocktail shaker with ice cubes.

Shake well.

Strain into a chilled cocktail glass.

Garnish with 3 Raspberries.

The part that makes this a "French " martini is the Chambord raspberry liqueur.

Although the FrenchMartini is not actually a Martini (due to the lack of vermouth), this is still a fantastic cocktail with just the right level of sweetness. Easy to drink with a fruity taste, it looks great too. In our opinion, the French Martini is everything a great cocktail should be and a staple of cocktail bars everywhere.

NIGHT OF ROSE

Ingredients
15 ml of liquor 43, 15 ml condensed milk, 20 ml espresso coffee, 40 ml of oat milk, 3 ounces of dark chocolate, 3 ounces whitechocolate

Preparation
The first thing we are going to prepare is the cream with oat milk and black and white chocolate. For this we put to heat in a saucepan the milk of oats and when it is very hot we remove it from the fire and we add the ounces of white chocolate and black chocolate. We remove all well so that the

chocolate is well melted and all well integrated. We booked it.

We also prepare an espresso so that it is cold at the moment we are going to use it. We booked it.

In our cocktail glasses we put the liquor43, the condensed milk, carefully used the back of a spoon to add our espresso and finally the cream that we have prepared with milk of oats and black and white chocolate. The cream can be beaten a bit to give it a creamier texture and it is also advisable to use the back of a spoon to add it to the cocktail.

You can sprinkle the cocktail with some grated coconut.

BLACKBERRY MULE

Ingredients
30 ml Vodka,
25 ml Crème de Mure,
25 ml Lime Juice,
Top-Up Ginger Beer, 6 Blackberries,
Aromatic Bitters

Preparation

Add 5 blackberries and lime juice into the mixing glass. Using a muddler press down the blackberries. Add vodka, creme de mure and dash of aromatic bitters. Add cubed ice and stir with a bar spoon, making sure to get to the bottom of the glass. Top up with ginger beer and give another stir. Top up with cubed ice, add a straw and garnish with blackberry.

A great cocktail in which the ginger beer adds a nice spicy dimension to the rich blackberry flavours.

A blackberry is not categorized as a berry but an aggregate fruit of numerous drupelets.

MINT JULEP

Ingredients

50 ml Knob Creek Bourbon,
bar spoon Granulated Sugar,
8 Mint leaves,
Mint sprigs

Preparation

Add a bar spoon of granulated sugar into the glass. Place 8 mint leaves into the glass and add 15 ml of Bourbon. Gently muddle contents of the glass. Add a further 35 ml of bourbon and then fill glass half way with crushed ice. Churn for 15 seconds and taste. Fill the remainder of the glass to the top with crushed ice. Slap mint sprigs to release flavour and add to the top of the drink. Place straw into the drink next to mint sprigs.

Since 1938, the Mint Julep has been promoted in association with the Kentucky Derby.

GRINCH

Ingredients

2 oz midori,
1/2 oz lemon, lime or pineapple juice,
1/4 oz simple syrup

Preparation

Fill a cocktail shaker with ice, and pour in all the ingredients. Shake well until chilled, and strain into a chilled martini glass. Garnish with a maraschino cherry.

This Grinch-colored cocktail is made with midori, a melon liqueur. It's sour and sweet and really refreshing to drink.

This drink makes a great afternoon pick me up. It can also make a good dessert drink if you're in the for something fruity. Midori always reminds me of the sort of really fruity drinks that we had as kids, so sometimes a Midori cocktail can bring back memories a more carefree time.

I almost wanted to call this this Fallout cocktail because it looks so radioactive, but I guess that's not very festive!

GIMLET

Ingredients

60 ml Premium Gin,
10 ml Lime Cordial

Preparation

Add gin and lime cordial to a mixing glass filled with ice. Stir to dilute and chill the drink. Strain into a cocktail glass and serve straight up.

The drink was named after British Royal Navy Surgeon General Sir Thomas D.Gimlette who allegedly introduced this drink as a means of inducing his messmates to take lime juice as an anti-scurvy medication.

SALTY DOG

Ingredients

50 ml Vodka,
20 ml Dry Sherry, 30
ml Grapefruit Juice,
15 ml Sugar Syrup,
Salt, Grapefruit Zest

Preparation

Prep a margarita glass by dipping half the rim in salt. Add all the ingredients to a cocktail shaker and shake with ice for about 10 seconds. Double strain into the salted glass. Zest the top of the drink with some grapefruit.

A superb combination with the grapefruit adding great depth to the gin.

In the Elmore Leonard novel "Swag", the Salty Dog is the preferred drink of honest and hard working career criminals Frank Ryan and Ernest Stickley Jnr.

RASPBERRY MOJITO

Ingredients
50 ml White Rum,
15 ml Raspberry Liqueur, 2
5 ml Lime Juice,
35 ml Soda Water,
2 Bar Spoons Superfine Sugar,
5 Raspberries,
8 Mint Leaves

Preparation

Add all your ingredients into a tall glass with crushed ice and churn, to dissolve the sugar and chill the drink. Top up with crushed ice. Add straw and garnish with raspberry.

A fruity twist on the classic Mojito cocktail, this is particularly good using fresh Scottish raspberries.

Raspberries come in many colors besides red: there are also black, purple and gold raspberries.

ACCOMPLICE

Ingredients

50 ml Vodka,
25 ml Lemon Juice,
15 ml Sugar Syrup,
Champagne,
3 Strawberries,

Preparation

Muddle 2 strawberries in a Boston Mixing
Glass. Add vodka, simple syrup and lemon
juice. Fill with ice and shake for 10 seconds.
Double strain into a chilled martini glass.
Top-up with Champagne and garnish the
glass with a strawberry.

A great Champagne cocktail which is sweet
and fruity and packs an unexpected kick.

The Accomplice cocktail tastes best with an
extra brut Champagne.

GIN RICKEY

Ingredients

50 ml Gin,
25 ml Lime Juice,
15 ml Sugar Syrup,
Soda Water,
Lime wedge

Preparation

Add all ingredients into Boston mixing tin, except the soda water. Fill the tin with ice and shake for about 10 seconds. Strain into a highball glass filled with ice and top up with soda water. Garnish with a wedge of lime.

:

A good alternative to the classic Gin & Tonic and perhaps even more refreshing.

By the 1890s the Gin Rickey had supplanted the early Bourbon version now known as the "Joe Rickey".

RAMOS GIN FIZZ

Ingredients

50 ml Gin,
25 ml Double Cream,
1 Egg White,
15 ml Lemon Juice or 15 ml Lime Juice, 20 ml Sugar Syrup, 4 drops Orange Flower Water, splash of Soda Water, Lemon Zest Twist.

Preparation

Add all ingredients into a shaker. Dry shake for 5 seconds. Add ice to the shaker and shake for up to 4 minutes to achieve the consistency desired for this drink. Add a dash of soda water to the bottom of a Collins glass and double strain the contents of the shaker into the glass. Zest the drink with a lemon twist and add it to the drink.

Quite a comprehensive cocktail recipe, where the egg white gives it body, the cream lends smoothness, and the citrus provides its cool. The soda wakes the whole drink up. Highly recommended.

The chief flavouring agent in gin is the highly aromatic blue-green berry of the juniper.

CAIPIRINHA

Ingredients
50 ml   Cachaça,
 1/2 Lime,
1 teaspoon   BrownSugar,   Lime Wedge

Preparation

Cut 1/2 lime into 1/8 ths and add half of these to Rocks glass. Add a teaspoon of brown sugar and muddle the ingredients. Add the rest of the lime and continue to muddle, to dissolve the sugar. Add the Cachaca and then add crushed ice on top. Stir to continue to dissolve the sugar. Add more crushed ice and continue to stir. Top up with crushed ice and garnish with lime wedge.

To make a Caipirinha you need Cachaca, and to make Cachaca you need sugar cane juice. Which is important, because it is what makes Cachaca a Cachaca, and not a rum. After that it follows a pretty similar path to rum, with the juice being fermented and then this liquid distilled. Sometimes the distilled liquid is popped in a barrel to go all smooth for sipping, but that's no good for a Caipirinha where it's all about the raw funky flavors.

The word Caipirinha is a diminutive version of the word caipira, which refers to someone from the countryside.

CHEEKY VIMTO

Ingredients
275 ml Blue Vodka WKD
50 ml   Port

Preparation
Mix both ingredients with ice in a pub glass.

Served neat or with ice, the very popular
Cheeky Vimto cocktail successfully recreates
both the flavour and colour of the popular
soft drink, so if you like Vimto you will
probably enjoy this drink. The Cheeky Vimto
first popped up in the UK about 2002 and
quickly became popular with a young and
boisterous crowd – for its sweet taste, novel
similarity to the popular soft drink and its
ability to get the drinker very drunk and very
quickly.
One aspect of this cocktail that surprises
people is that it actually does not contain
Vimto as one of its ingredients. Vimto is a soft
drink which was originally created in England.
It was originally produced as a health tonic,

around 1908, but went on to become a carbonated drink several decades later. Vimto contains the juice of raspberries, blackcurrants, grapes and various herbs and spices.

There have been several other cocktails created with the aim of mimicking a popular soft drink, perhaps the most famous being the Flaming Dr.Pepper, which is a potent mix of beer, Amaretto and Everclear. The addition of the Everclear, which is a very high proof spirit, enables the cocktail to be set alight.

You can also create a variation of the Cheeky Vimto called the Extra Cheeky Vimto, which replaces one of the shots of port with a shot of vodka. This drink has become increasingly popular at college events and other occasions which can get a bit "rowdy", such as hen parties and stage events.

A variant, Extra Cheeky Vimto, replaces one of the port shots with neat vodka.

SINGAPORE SLING

Ingredients
35 ml   Gin,

15 ml   Cherry Heering,

15 ml   Benedictine,

25 ml   Lemon Juice,

2 dashes   Orange Bitters,

2 dashes   Angostura   Bitters,

dash   Soda Water, Lemon slice

Preparation
Chill highball glass with soda water. Add all ingredients into mixing tin and fill with ice. Shake hard for 10 seconds. Taste. Top up the highball glass with ice and single strain the drink into glass. Top up with soda water, add straw and garnish with   lemon slice.

This is a sweet cocktail with quite a complex flavour. Not for novices.

The   Singapore   Sling is a cocktail that was developed sometime before 1915 by Ngiam

Tong Boon, a bartender working at the "Long Bar" in Raffles Hotel Singapore.

ALASKA COCKTAIL

Ingredient
35 ml   Gin,
20 ml   Yellow Chartreuse,
3 drops Orange   Bitters,
Orange   ZestTwist

Preparation
Add all ingredients into a mixing glass filled with ice. Stir with a bar spoon to dilute and chill the drink. Pour into a cocktail glass and zest the drink and the glass using an   orange zest   twist. Serve straight up.

A very unique-tasting combination, which is strong and bursting with   zesty, aromatic flavours. Definitely worth a try.

Yellow Chartreuse has a milder, sweeter flavour than its green equivalent.

MOJITO

Ingredients
50 ml White   Rum,
8 Mint leaves,
15 ml Sugar Syrup,
25 ml Lime Juice,
2 Mint sprigs

Preparation
Add the   whiterum to a highball glass. Add 8
– 10   mint leaves and   sugar syrup and   lime
juice. Muddle with a bar spoon. Add crushed
ice and a splash of soda. Mix the drink down
with a bar spoon. Taste. Top up with more
crushed ice. Slap 2 mint sprigs to release
essence and put into drink. Add a small splash
of soda and straw.

If there is one cocktail to divide opinion, it is
surely the omnipresent Mojito cocktail. Some
say it is a pain in the arse to make, is too
frequently made badly, and is the mascot for
unadventurous drinkers everywhere. Others
say it is a refreshing and easy drinking cocktail

that has introduced millions to the wonders of the mixed drink. Whatever side of the fence you sit on, it's certainly helped line the pockets of a few mint-growers.

Cuba is where the Mojito cocktail calls home, although whether it came about through the experimentations of African slaves in the 1800s, or was created by the explorer-cum-pirate-cum-mixologist Richard Drake way back in the 1500s is a matter for the historians to concern themselves with. Either way it wasn't long before Bacardi saw the potential of this cocktail to market their rum, and the two have been synonymous ever since; helped of course by that most respected of inebriates Hemingway, who is said to have developed a taste during a visit to the bar La Bodeguita del Medio in Cuba.

Despite its ubiquitous nature, the Mojito is a tricky scoundrel to make well. First up you'll be needing to muddle the mint, but treat it too roughly and it'll get its own back by releasing a torrent of bitter flavors into your drink. The trick is to use plenty of leaves (a good dozen), clap between your hands (they like being praised) and then barely tickle them with the muddler (or rolling pin) in the base of your chosen glass. Next up is the lime, about ¾ of a shot depending on how sour they happen to be on the day. Too many recipes call for sugar, but unless you have the patience of a saint to ensure it is properly dissolved before drinking, it's best to stick with sugar syrup, about half a shot's worth. It's the balance of mint, lime and sugar that is key to the success of this drink and it's worth a bit of practice. A double shot of white rum comes next, preferably something with some flavour. Havana Club 3yr is widely available and a solid choice, or else El Dorado 3yr is worth seeking out for a creamier and more coconut-led flavour. Crushed ice comes next; if you only have lumpy ice then it's time to get a cloth out to wrap it up and whack it with something heavy. Pop a load in the glass, churn it up a bit, add some more and a splash of soda (not too much) and stir some more. Hey presto you have a drink that took longer to make than it will to drink!

If you fancy something a bit more exotic then there are options galore. You could sub the sugar syrup for all manner of liqueurs from apple liqueur, to Grand Mariner or St Germain elderflower for a fruitier treat for instance. Pluck for an aged rum for a deeper flavour, or do away with the rum altogether, soju works well for instance. My secret? Add just a dash of absinthe, it'll make you feel all perky.

WHITE RUSSIAN

Ingredients
35 ml Vodka,
25 ml Coffee Liqueur,
15 ml Cream,
15 ml Milk,
Chocolate Powder,
Coffee Beans

Preparation
For the perfect White Russian recipe add coffee liqueur to an old-fashioned glass. Add other ingredients to mixing tin and fill to brim

with ice. Shake for 10 -15 seconds. Single strain the ingredients over the ice and coffee liqueur. Sprinkle it with   chocolate powder and garnish with   coffee beans.

This   White   Russian recipe is one of the most popular of all cocktails, and with good reason. It has a deep, smooth flavour and is the perfect drink to kick back and relax with.

The White Russian is the favourite drink of Jeffrey "The Dude" Lebowski, the main character of the 1998 film, "The Big Lebowski".

ESPRESSO   MARTINI

Ingredients
35 ml   Vanilla   Vodka,
15ml   Kahlúa,
 Double Espresso,
15ml Sugar Syrup,
3 Coffee Beans

Preparation

Add all ingredients into a Boston cocktail shaker and fill with ice. Shake hard for up to 30 seconds to achieve the desired consistency of the drink. Double strain the contents of the shaker into a chilled martini glass. Garnish with 3 coffee beans.

A silky smooth martini with that caffeinated kick to keep the night going that extra hour longer!

Coffee is the second most traded commodity on earth.

PALOMA

Ingredients

50 ml Tequila, 27 1/2 ml Pink Grapefruit Juice, 20 ml Sugar Syrup, 10 ml Lime Juice, Pink Grapefruit wedge

Preparation

Chill highball glass. Add all ingredients into highball and fill to brim with ice. Stir with a bar spoon for 10 seconds. Top up with fresh ice and top up with soda. Add straw and garnish with a wedge of pink grapefruit.

A light, fruity drink, which is an ideal thirst quencher. One of our favourite tequila cocktails.

The Paloma is the most popular tequila based cocktail in Mexico

TEQUILA SUNRISE

Ingredients
50 ml Tequila,
80 ml Orange Juice,
dash Grenadine Syrup,
Lime wedge,
 Orange slice.

Preparation
Add tequila into highball glass. Top up with ice. Add freshly squeezed   orange juice , squeeze of lime and dash of grenadine syrup.

The Tequila Sunrise is a popular and refreshing tequila-based cocktail which is made with tequila, orange juice and grenadine syrup. The cocktail was originally made with tequila, crème de cassis, lime juice and soda water but the recipe has evolved over the years. The cocktail is most famous for its sunrise appearance which is created by pouring the grenadine syrup into the drink over a spoon, with the aim of as little mixing as possible.

As is the case with nearly all iconic cocktails, the origins of the Tequila Sunrise cocktail is not without debate. The most popular story tracing the birth of the drink credits a barman called Gene Sulit who worked at the luxurious Arizona Biltmore Hotel during the 1930's. Another story was that it was created at the Agua Caliente of Tijuana, Mexico in the post-Prohibition era as many wealthy Americans headed south to gamble and party.

The popularity of the Tequila Sunrise cocktail has launched many variations of the cocktail, such as the Caribbean Sunrise, which uses rum instead of tequila, the Amaretto Sunrise, which uses amaretto instead of tequila and the nonalcoholic Red Sea Sunrise that uses lemonade instead of tequila.

Tequila Sunrise, featuring Mel Gibson, holds a score of 44% on Rotten Tomatoes.

DARK STORMY

Ingredients
50 ml Dark Rum,
4 Lime quarters,
1 1/2 bar spoons Brown Sugar,
splash Ginger Beer,
Lime wedge.

Preparation
Chill highball glass with soda water. Place 4 lime quarters into mixing tin and add 1 1/2 bar spoons of brown sugar. Muddle ingredients. Add 50 ml of dark rum. Fill the mixing tin with ice and shake hard for 10 – 15

seconds. Taste. Add fresh ice to the highball glass and single strain drink over the ice. Top up with   ginger beer and add straw. Garnish with lime wedge.

:

A great tropical concoction in which the sweetness of the rum and   ginger is cut with the tart of the lime.

This drink gained popularity through the sailing community up and down the east coast of the USA, having been brought home by various sailors who visited Bermuda.

NEGRONI

Ingredients
30 ml   Gin,
30 ml Sweet Red Vermouth,
30 ml   Campari,
Orange Peel.

Preparation
Chill rocks glass with ice and soda water. Fill mixing tin to rim with ice and add in all

ingredients. Stir with a bar spoon for 20 seconds. Taste. Add fresh ice to rocks glass and strain the drink into glass. Zest glass with orange peel, twist and place in drink.

Like fashion, cocktail culture has its ups and downs. We've raunchy-named garish tooth-rotters, and we've had the uninspired vodka revolution. It was only a matter of time therefore, that bitterness came back on the menu, and with it, the rise in popularity of its ambassador the Negroni.

Taking its name from Count Camillo Negroni, the Negroni was created at the Casoni bar in Florence as a result of the bartender being asked for an Americano with a bit more kick; the Americano being equal parts Campari Bitter and Sweet Vermouth topped with soda. Subbing the soda for Gin (using the same amount as the vermouth and Campari) was a move of frankly genius proportions, for this is one of the most remarkably tasty cocktails known to mankind. Except for most new recruits it isn't, bitterness is this drink's forte, and bitter it certainly is.

As with many classic cocktails, the Negroni has attracted plenty of fiddling over the years. The substitution of Campari with Aperol being a common twist, resulting in a far less bitter drink, and hence much more quaffable. The Italians, insistent upon moving the drink back towards its routes, created the Negroni Sbagliato (wrong Negroni) by doing away with the gin and adding in sparkling wine. It's an improvement on the Americano for sure, but not of the Negroni. That's the trouble with Italian's not being able to handle their booze, they go for the light stuff. Of course all manner of other spirits, Amari and bitters can be used in place of the classic ingredients but there are two that really stand out. Substitute gin for bourbon and you have yourself a Boulevardier; sweeter and more deeply flavoured than its sibling, it's hard to go back to the gin-based stuff afterwards. To come bang up to date however, you'll be wanting to do away with the Campari and replace it with Kamm and Sons, a bitter-tasting ginseng spirit made with so many botanicals it's almost certain to be good for you.

Making one of these is easy-freakin'-peasy. Pop as many ice cubes as you can fit into a rocks glass. Add a measure each of gin, sweet vermouth and Campari then stir, a bit. Not too much or by the time you've finished the drink it'll be all weak and lifeless, and this is supposed to be a big bold libation. Add yourself a fat wedge/slice of orange for a garnish and you're sorted. Except for the antipasti, for this is a drink that will stimulate the appetite if ever there was one.

Legend has it that Count Camillio Negroni invented this drink by asking his bartender to strengthen his favourite drink, Americano, by adding gin rather than the normal soda water.

JOHN COLLINS

Ingredients
50 ml Bourbon Whiskey,
25 ml Lemon Juice,

15 ml Sugar Syrup, splash of Soda Water, Maraschino Cherry.

Preparation
Mix the Bourbon, lemon juice and sugar syrup in a Boston shaker with ice. Single strain into a highball glass filled with ice. Top up with soda water. Garnish with maraschino cherry.

Another popular variation of the Tom Collins, this is a tasty bourbon sour that makes a great summer evening mixed drink.

The Bourbon name was derived from Bourbon county, a large Kentucky county founded after the American Revolution.

EL DIABLO

Ingredients
35 ml Tequila,
15 ml Crème de Cassis,
15 ml Lime Juice,
Ginger Beer

Preparation

Pour the tequila, cassis, and lime juice into a cocktail shaker filled with ice. Shake well. Strain into a Collins glass filled with ice. Top with ginger beer.

A popular tequila cocktail with the cassis melding perfectly with the ginger and the agave flavour of the tequila. This has long been a favourite cocktail of ours and looks great due to the way the cassis dissolves into the drink, creating a purple haze.

The earliest reference to the El Diablo cocktail can be found in the Cocktail Recipe books of Tiki legend Trader Vic. In his 1946 "Book of Food and Drink" it is referred to as a "Mexican El Diablo" but whether it was an original Trader Vic cocktail or not remains unclear.

The EL Diablo appeared in Trader Vics "Book of Food and Drink" as early as 1946.

CLOVER CLUB

Ingredients
35 ml   Gin,
35 ml   Lemon Juice,
20 ml Sweet   Vermouth,
20 ml   Raspberry Syrup,
1 Egg White,

Preparation
Pour the ingredients into a cocktail shaker and dry shake for 5 seconds. Add ice to the shaker and shake hard for a further 15 seconds. Single strain into a coupe glass and serve.

This is a fruity and well balanced cocktail, with the raspberry syrup bringing the whole concoction to life. Looks great as well.

The egg white in this drink is not added for the purposes of giving the drink flavour,but rather acts as an emulsifier. Thus, when the drink is shaken, a characteristic foamy head is formed.

B52

Ingredients
10 ml Coffee Liqueur, 10 ml Irish Cream
Liqueur, 10 ml Triple Sec

Preparation
Layer ingredients into a shot glass. Serve with
a stirrer.

The B-52 cocktail is a popular layer shot made
from   coffee liqueur,   Irishcream   liqueur
and   triple sec. When the shot is prepared
properly the three ingredients will separate
into three distinct layers due to the different
densities of the alcohols. The combination of
coffee and Irish cream liqueur has always been
popular and the addition of the fruity edge
that the triple sec brings adds an extra tasty
dimension to this cocktail shooter.
The exact origins of the B-52, like most
famous cocktails, are disputed. One story is
that the drink was created at the well-known
Alice's restaurant in Malibu in the late 1960`s
and was named after the famous fighter plane

that was predominantly used in the Vietnam War. One theory was that the orange liqueur at the top of the shot was a metaphor for a downed plane that had burst into flames. Another theory was that the B-52 was invented by Peter Fich who was the head bartender at the Banff Springs Hotel in Alberta. The story goes that he named all his new drinks after his favourite bands and hence this was named after the popular American band of the same name.

Although the B-52 is usually built in a shot glass, it is sometimes shaken and served in a cocktail glass. Several variations on the drink exist, such as the B-51, which uses Frangelico instead of Triple Sec and the B-53 which uses Sambuca rather than Irish Cream liqueur. Other more elaborate variations include the B-52 Gunship, which uses Absinthe instead of the triple sec and B-52 in the Desert which replaces Irish Cream liqueur with tequila.

B-52 carries up to 70,000 pounds of weapons.

VOLCANO

Ingredients

125 ml Golden Rum, 25 ml Dark Rum, 10 ml 151 Rum, 6 dashes Absinthe, 6 dashes Angostura Bitters, 50 ml Pink Grapefruit Juice, 50 ml Orange Juice, 50 ml Pineapple Juice, 50 ml Lime Juice, 25 ml Falernum, 50 ml Grenadine Syrup, Cinnamon

Preparation

Add all ingredients (except 151 proof rum) into a large mixing glass filled with ice. Stir with a bar spoon for 15 seconds. Pour into a mixing bowl or a volcano bowl if you have one available. Top with crushed ice. Pout on 151 proof rum and set light. Sprinkle cinnamon over the drink to garnish.

The ultimate group cocktail, this Tiki-style concoction is an explosion of tropical flavours and is extremely boozy, so be careful!

Some claim that the Volcano came from Chile during the times of Augusto Pinochet.

SCREWDRIVER

Ingredients
50 ml Vodka,
100 ml freshly squeezed Orange Juice,
Lime wedge

Preparation
Add   vodka into highball glass and fill up to
the top with ice. Squeeze a lime wedge into
the drink and rim glass. Top up with freshly
squeezed orange juice. Add straw and serve.

Straightforward combination of a spirit and
fresh fruit juice. Always a safe choice.

This drink got its name because American
petroleum engineers in Saudi Arabia secretly
added vodka to small cans of orange juice and
stirred the mixture with their screwdrivers.

PAIN KILLER

Ingredients
50 ml Dark Rum, 25 ml Coconut Cream,
100 ml Pineapple Juice, 25 ml Orange
Juice, Orange Wheel

Preparation
Add all ingredients into a mixing tin and top-up with cubed ice. Shake hard for 10 seconds. Fill a tall glass with crushed ice and strain mixture into glass. Garnish with orange wheels.

A fantastic Tiki-style rum concoction featuring the trusted flavours of coconut and pineapple. We love this drink.

"Painkiller" is a 1990 gold-certified album by British heavy metal band Judas Priest.

WOOWOO

Ingredients
35 ml Peach Schnapps,
35 ml Vodka,
90 ml Cranberry Juice

Preparation
Pour all ingredients into a highball glass over ice cubes, stir with a bar spoon for 15 seconds and serve.

A popular and fun cocktail. If you are looking for "easy to drink" and not too concerned with sophistication, the Woo Woo, not unlike a Sex on the Beach, is a perfect choice.

A Woo Woo is a "Sex on the Beach" without the orange juice.

BUCKS FIZZ

Ingredients
50 ml Orange Juice,
100 ml Champagne,

Preparation

Pour 50 ml of orange juice into Champagne flute. Using a bar spoon, float Champagne on top. Lightly stir to combine.

The Bucks Fizz cocktail is a popular wedding cocktail which is two parts Champagne and one part orange juice. In the past this cocktail also included grenadine syrup, but rarely does today. The Bucks Fizz cocktail is very similar to another popular cocktail called the Mimosa, with the only difference being that the Mimosa is equal parts Champagne and orange juice.

The Bucks Fizz cocktail was created at The Bucks Club in London where in the 1920`s legend it was created as an early morning/ brunch cocktail. The original recipe apparently featured additional ingredients than Champagne and orange juice and was created by a bartender called McGarry. Since then bartenders have looked to give the cocktail an extra kick of flavour by adding such ingredients as gin and Peter Heering cherry liqueur.

Bucks Fizz is popularly served at weddings as a less alcoholic alternative to Champagne.

EL PRESIDENTE

Ingredients
50 ml Aged Rum,
15 ml Orange Liqueur,
10 ml Dry Vermouth,
splash Grenadine,
Orange Peel

Preparation
Begin by chilling coupe glass with ice and soda. Add ice to the mixing glass and add all ingredients. Stir sown the drink for 20 seconds, using a bar spoon. When mixing ensure the glass is kept full to the brim with ice. Strain the drink into the chilled coupe glass and serve straight up. Garnish with orange peel twist.

Rum and orange combine beautifully in our favourite Daiquiri concoction.

A Cuban creation, El Presidente was the house cocktail at Club El Chico in Manhattan's Greenwich village, where America was introduced to the rhumba in 1925.

RUM RUNNER

Ingredients
35 ml Aged Rum,
20 ml White Rum,
15 ml Creme de Banane,
10 ml Creme de Mure,
15 ml Pineapple Juice,
15 ml Orange Juice,
Orange slice

Preparation
Chill down rocks glass with ice and soda. Add all ingredients into the mixing tin. Add ice to the mixing tin and shake hard for 10 seconds. Add fresh ice into rocks glass and strain the drink into the glass. Garnish with orange slices.

A very smooth and sweet tasting cocktail which goes down easily, but still has a kick.

Bacardi is the world's most popular brand of rum.

MAITAI

Ingredients
20 ml Dark Rum,
20 ml Light Rum,
20 ml Triple Sec,
20 ml Lime Juice,
10 ml Orgeat Syrup,
Mint sprig,
Orange wedge

Preparation
Add all ingredients into the mixing tin. Fill mixing tin with cubed ice. Shake very hard for 10 seconds to achieve desired dilution. Fill goblet style glass with crushed ice and strain mixture into glass. Add a short straw, mint and a splash of demerara rum.

For many this is the king of Tiki-style drinks.A beautiful fruity concoction which deserves to use the best quality rums you can find.

The Mai-Tai was prominently featured in the popular Elvis Presley film "Blue Hawaii".

BLACK RUSSIAN

Ingredients
45 ml Vodka,
25 ml Coffee Liqueur

Preparation
Add vodka and coffee liqueur to rocks glass. Fill the glass with ice. Stir for 5 seconds with a bar spoon. Top up with ice and serve.

This is the perfect coffee-flavoured cocktail for novices. Easy to make and will suit nearly all tastes. Its popularity is well deserved.

This drink can be topped with cola and it is then referred to as the Dirty Black Russian.

BLACK STRIPE

Ingredients
50 ml Dark Rum,
1 teaspoon Honey, Hot Water, Lemon Twist, Cinnamon Stick

Preparation
Pour the dark rum and honey into an Irish coffee glass. Twist a lemon twist over the glass and drop it into the glass. Fill the glass with hot water. Garnish with cinnamon sticks.

A delicious winter warmer in which the honey pairs perfectly with the hot rum.

Every pattern on a zebra is unique.

BLOODY MARGARET

Ingredient
45 ml Gin ,
90 ml Tomato Juice,
15 ml Lemon Juice,
1 dash Tabasco Sauce,
2 dashes Worcestershire Sauce,
1 dash Salt,
1 dash Pepper,
Celery Stalk

Preparation
Add dashes of Worcestershire Sauce, Tabasco, salt and pepper into highball glass, then pour all ingredients into highball with ice cubes. Stir gently. Garnish with celery stalk.

This is a variation of the Bloody Mary using gin instead of vodka, which adds a nice earthy edge to the classic drink.

Margaret Thatcher's favourite tipple was Bell's Whisky.

BLUSHING BRIDE

Ingredients
25 ml Peach Schnapps, 100 ml Champagne,
25 ml Grenadine Syrup

Preparation
Pour the peach schnapps and grenadine syrup
into a Champagne flute. Top-up with
Champagne.

The real charm of this Champagne cocktail is
the amazing blush colour that is created.
Perfect for a wedding toast.

Approximately 49 million bubbles can be
found in a 750ml champagne bottle that is
stored at 20 C.

BRAMBLE

Ingredients
50 ml Gin,
10 ml Crème de Mûre,
25 ml Lemon Juice,

15 ml Sugar Syrup,
Blackberry

Preparation
Add all ingredients (except creme de mure)
into mixing glass. Fill mixing glass with cubed
ice and fill rocks glass with crushed ice. Shake
for 10 seconds. Strain mixture into glass and
top up with crushed ice. Pour creme de mure
over the drink using a bar spoon. Garnish
with 2 lemon slices and blackberry.

The pairing of the gin, blackberry and lemon
comes together to create a light tasting and
refreshing cocktail which has long been one of
our favourites at Social and Cocktail HQ.

The Bramble was invented by Dick Bradsell in
1984 at Fred's Club in London's SOHO.

MANY OTHER RECIPES OF DELICIOUS COCKTAILS

Kryptonite

Ingredients:
2.3 cl Light Rum
2.3 cl Midori Melon Liqueur
3 cl Pineapple Juice
3 cl Sprite

Mixture:
1. Pour all ingredients but the soda into a cocktail shaker filled with ice.
2. Shake and strain into an old-fashioned glass with ice.
3. Top with Sprite.
4. Serve.

Dubonnet Fizz

Ingredients:
3 cl Cherry Liqueur
3 cl Dubonnet
3 cl Orange Juice
1.5 cl Lemon Juice
Soda Water
Mixture:
1. Pour all ingredients, except soda water, into a cocktail shaker filled with ice.
2. Shake and strain into a highball glass.
3. Top with soda water.
4. Garnish with a lemon slice and a red cherry.
5. Serve.

Airattack

Ingredients:
2 cl Calvados
2 cl Gin
2 cl Brandy
2 cl Absinthe
2 cl Peach Liqueur
2 cl Sekt

6 cl Cherry Juice

Mixture:
1. Shake all ingredients (except Sekt) with ice.
2. Pour into a highball glass.
3. Top with Sekt.
4. Garnish with a cherry.

Fallen Angel

Ingredients:
5 cl Gin
1 Dash Angostura Bitter
2 cl Advocaat
2 drops Creme de Menthe White
2 cl Kirsch
1 Lemon (Juice)
Lemonade

Mixture:
1. Fill a highball glass with ice.
2. Pour all ingredients into the highball glass.
3. Garnish with a cherry.
4. Serve.

Kingston

Ingredients:
1.5 cl Gin
2.5 cl Rum Spiced
2.5 cl Lime Juice
3 Dashes Grenadine Syrup
Mixture:
1. Pour all ingredients into a cocktail shaker with crushed ice.
2. Shake and strain into a cocktail glass.
3. Serve.

Kiss on the Lips

Ingredients:
15 cl Frozen Mango Mix
4.5 cl Peach Schnapps
1 Tablespoon Grenadine Syrup

Mixture:
1. Pour Peach schnapps and mango mix into a blender and blend with crushed ice.
2. Place the Grenadine syrup in a cocktail glass.

3. Pour the mix over the grenadine syrup.
4. Serve.

Kaalis Envy

Ingredients:
1.5 cl Tequila
4.5 cl Midori Melon Liqueur
1.5 cl, Vanilla Liqueur
Pineapple

Mixture:
1. Put 5-6 pineapple pieces in a cocktail shaker and crush it.
2. Add ice, midori, tequila and vanilla liqueur.
3. Shake and pour into a hurricane glass.
4. Garnish with a piece of pineapple.
5. Serve.

Kahlua Mint slide

Ingredients:
3/4 oz, Coffee Liqueur (Kahlua)
1/2 oz Green Creme de Menthe
1/2 oz White Creme de Cacao

Milk
Whipped Cream - to top
Cookie - for garnish
1 cup Ice
Garnish: Cookie
Glass: Highball Glass

Whipped Iced Milk

Ingredients
2 oz Coffee Liqueur (Kahlua)
1 oz Milk
2 oz Coffee - chilled
1 oz Whipped Cream Vodka (Pinnacle)
Whipped Cream - to top
Glass: Highball Glass

Upside Down Hypnotic

Ingredients
2 oz Hpnotiq
1/2 oz Vodka
1 splash Pineapple Juice
1 splash Grenadine
Garnish: Pineapple

Glass: Rocks Glass

Esme's Peril

Ingredients:
9 cl White Rum
3 cl Dark Rum
2 Tablespoons Banana Liqueur
6 cl Lemon Juice
3 cl Orange Juice
3 Tablespoons Cream
2 Teaspoons Sugar granulated
1/2 Banana
4 Strawberry(s)

Mixture:
1. Pour all ingredients into a cocktail shaker with ice..
2. Shake and strain into a beer mug.
3. Garnish with banana.
4. Serve.

Cheeky Girl

Ingredients:

1.5 cl Malibu Coconut Rum
1.5 cl Cognac
3 cl Banana Liqueur
3 cl Kahlua
6 cl Cream

Mixture:
1. Pour all ingredients into a cocktail shaker with ice.
2. Shake and strain into a wine glass with ice.
3. Garnish with a banana slice.
4. Serve.

Afterglow

Ingredients:
12 cl Pineapple Juice
12 cl Orange Juice
3 cl Grenadine Syrup

Mixture:
1. Pour the grenadine and juices into a cocktail shaker and mix them together.
2. Pour into a highball glass with ice.
3. Garnish with a pineapple chunk.

4. Serve

2 B Slippery

Ingredients:
3 cl Black Sambuca
3 cl Lime Liqueur

Mixture:
1. Pour the ingredients into a lowball glass and add some ice cubes.
2. Serve

Lambada

Ingredients:
1.5 cl Tequila
1.5 cl Mango Liqueur
1.5 cl Black Sambuca

Mixture:
1. Layer in order in a shooter glass using the back of a bar spoon.
2. Serve.

Nightmare

Ingredients:
1.5 cl Rumple Minze
1.5 cl 151-proof Rum
1.5 cl Goldschlager
1.5 cl Jägermeister

Mixture

1. Pour all ingredients into a cocktail shaker filled with ice.
2 Shake and strain into a shooter glass.
3. Serve.

B&G

Ingredients:
3 cl Benedictine herbal liqueur
3 cl Grand Marnier
Mixture:
1. Pour all ingredients into a lowball glass with ice.
2. Serve.

Brutus

Ingredients:
4.5 cl Vodka
1.5 cl Cynar
3 cl Sweet Vermouth

Mixture:
1. Pour all ingredients into a cocktail shaker with ice.
2. Shake and strain into a highball glass with ice.
3. Serve.

Lotus Cocktail

Ingredientes
7 Mint leaves
60 ml Gin
7.5 ml Blue curaçao liqueur
30 ml Lychee juice drink
7.5 ml Grenadine/pomegranate syrup

Red Rum 'Martini'

Ingredientes
24 Red currants
60 ml Rum - 6-10yr old Caribbean blended
rum
15 ml Sloe Gin liqueur
15 ml Lemon juice (freshly squeezed)
15 ml Vanilla sugar syrup

Le Grand Sunset

Ingredients
1 oz Vodka
1 oz Grand Marnier
4 oz Orange Juice
1 dash Grenadine

Midori Colada

Ingredients:
3 cl White Rum
6 cl Midori Melon Liqueur
12 cl Pineapple Juice
6 cl Coconut Cream

Mixture:
1. Pour all ingredients into a blender. 2. Pour into a Hurricane glass. 3. Serve with a straw.

Alligator

Ingredients:
6 cl Midori Melon Liqueur
12 cl Orange Juice

Mixture:
1. Fill glass half-way with Ice.
2. Add Midori and Orange Juice.
3. Stir and Serve.

Banana Mango

Ingredients:
4.5 cl Light Rum
0.8 cl Banana Liqueur
1.5 cl Mango Nectar
1.5 cl Lime Juice

Mixture:
1. Fill cocktail shaker with ice.

2. Add all ingredients.
3. Shake and strain into a chilled old-fashioned glass with ice.
4. Serve.

Astronaut

Ingredients:
4.5 cl Jamaica Rum
4.5 cl Vodka
1 1/2 Teaspoon Passion Fruit Juice
1 1/2 Teaspoon Lemon Juice

Mixture:
1. Fill cocktail shaker with ice.
2. Pour all ingredients into the cocktail shaker and shake.
3. Strain into a Collins glass with ice.
4. Serve

Banana Berry
Ingredients:
4.5 cl Creme de Banana
2 Dashes Grenadine Syrup
Milk

Mixture:
1. Fill a highball glass with ice.
2. Pour crème de banane over the ice.
3. Top with Milk and finally add the Grenadine.
4. Serve.

Shirley Temple Champagne

Ingredientes
1 oz grenadine
6 oz champagne
maraschino cherries (for garnish)

Thyme to Delight

Ingredientes
45 mL Strawberry-infused Aviation Gin
30 mL Fresh Lemon Juice
15 mL House-made Thyme & Hibiscus Syrup
Egg White

Fig Sidecar

Ingredientes
1 ounce cognac (we used Hennessy)
1 1/2 ounce fresh squeezed lemon juice
1/2 ounce cointreau
3/4 ounce fig syrup (find the how-to in the
post)
1 ripe fig

The Sleeping Beauty Cocktail

Ingredientes
3 oz. (90ml) Hpnotiq
2 oz. (60ml) Kinky Pink Liqueur
2 oz. (60ml) Vodka
1 oz. (30ml) Lemon Lime Soda

Pink Lady

Ingredientes
40 ml Gin
40 ml Grenadine
20 ml Cream
1 Egg white

Pink Poodle

Ingredients
45 ml Smirnoff vodka
80ml Pineapple juice
20 Strawberry Crush
Half scoop Vanilla Ice Cream
Garnish – Pineapple / Strawberry Slice
Glass – Tall

Pineapple Margarita

This pineapple Margarita is the perfect fruity alcoholic drink for summer. Pineapple and lime juices ...

Ingredientes
3 ounces pineapple juice
1 ounce lime juice
1 1/2 ounces tequila
3/4 ounce triple sec
1 teaspoon simple syrup (optional)

Green Margarita

This twist on the classic Margarita recipe uses a delicious sugar snap pea puree.

Ingredientes
1 1/2 ounces blanco tequila
1/2 ounce Combier
1/2 ounce St-Germain
3/4 ounce lime juice, freshly squeezed
1 ounce pea purée

Green Hope

Ingredients:
3 cl Vodka (Cossack)
1/2 cl Green Curacao (Bols)
1/2 cl Creme de Banane (Bols)
1/2 cl Grapefruit juice
1 1/2 cl Lemon juice

Mixing instructions:
Shake with ice. Garnish with red and red cherries.

Black Eye

A fruity Rusty Nail variation.
Ingredientes
2 Blackberries
5 Raspberries (fresh)
5 Mint leaves
60 ml Irish whiskey
22.5 ml Drambuie liqueur

Black and Tan

The black and tan is a popular beer drink of Guinness layered on top of Bass ale. Find tips for ...

Ingredientes
6 ounces pale ale beer
6 ounces Guinness stout beer

Irish Lady

Ingredientes
1½ ounces Irish Whiskey
½ ounce triple sec

1 ounce lemon juice
½ ounce simple syrup
1 egg white

Jack in Black

Ingredientes
45 ml Whiskey - Tennessee whiskey
22.5 ml Coffee liqueur
105 ml Cola

Irish Buck

Ingredientes
1 1/2 ounces Irish whiskey
1/4 ounce lime juice, freshly squeezed
2 ounces ginger ale, to top
Garnish: lime wheel

Blush Ruby Rush

Ingredients
2 ounce Ziami Ruby Rush Rum
2 whole strawberry

½ ounce (s) Freshly squeezed lemon juice
top off with Water - Soda from Siphon

Nobody Puts Baby in the Corner

Ingredients
1.5 oz Woodford Reserve rye whiskey
1 oz PAMA liqueur
0.75 oz lemon juice
0.75 oz simple syrup
1 egg white

China Blue

Looks sweet, but due to a generous splash of
grapefruit is actually balanced and refreshing.

Ingredientes
30 ml Lychee liqueur
30 ml Blue curaçao liqueur
120 ml Grapefruit juice (pink)

South Pacific Breeze

Ingredientes
45 ml Gin
22.5 ml Galliano L'Autentico liqueur
Soda limon/Sprite/7-up
22.5 ml Licor Blue Curaçao

Blue Heaven

Ingredientes
60 ml Rum - White (charcoal-filtered) 1-3
year old light
15 ml Amaretto liqueur
30 ml Licor Blue Curaçao
15 ml Cordial Rose's Lime
120 ml Suco fresco de Abacaxi

Blue Passion

Ingredientes
30 ml Rum - White (charcoal-filtered) 1-3
year old light
30 ml Licor Blue Curaçao
52.5 ml Suco fresco de Limão

30 ml Sugar syrup (2:1)

Blue Goose Drink

Ingredientes
1 ounce Hpnotiq
1 ounce Grey Goose vodka
Lime juice
1 1/2 ounces orgeat syrup

Old Jamaican

Respect your elders with this delicious rum drink. Check out the Old Jamaican cocktail recipe.
Ingredientes
1 sprig Mint, Fresh
3/4 oz Cane simple syrup, Pure
1 oz Lime juice, Fresh
1 dash Angostura bitters
1 1/2 oz Appleton estate reserve rum

Dutch Mule

Ginger spice invigorates this long refreshing cocktail with a splash of genever adding to the Dutch ...
Ingredientes
45 ml Vodka
15 ml Genever - Oude genever
22.5 ml Suco fresco de Limão
3 Angostura or other aromatic bitters
90 ml Ginger beer

Mexican mule

Tequila-based Moscow Mule.
Ingredients
60 ml Tequila reposata
15 ml Fresh lemon juice
10 ml of sugar syrup (2: 1)
90 ml ginger beer

Jamaican mule

Long rum-based drink with a spicy ginger flavor.

Ingredients
60ml Rum - Spicy
15 ml Fresh lemon juice
10 ml of sugar syrup (2: 1)
90 ml ginger beer

Berlin Sour

Ingredientes
60 ml Kummel liqueur
15 ml Maraschino liqueur
30 ml Lemon juice (freshly squeezed)
7.5 ml Sugar syrup (2:1)
Flirting   2
Easy to drink
Ingredients
22.5 ml vodka
22.5 ml Triple sec
60 ml Fresh pineapple juice
Champagne Brut

Simple Truth

Ingredientes
60 ml Bacardi Carta Blanca

3/4 Pineapple juice (fresh pressed)

15 ml Honey sugar syrup

15 ml Grapefruit juice (pink)

10 ml Campari or other red bitter liqueur

Cowboy Hoof Martini

Lightly sweetened gin shaken with fresh aromatic mint.

Ingredientes

5 Mint Leaves

75 ml Gin

5 ml Sugar syrup (2:1)

2 Orange bitters (optional)

Black Diamond

This flavoursome mix of coffee and chocolate is further enhanced if vanilla-infused rum is used.

Ingredientes

30 ml Rum - White (charcoal-filtered) 1-3 year old light

30 ml Dark crème de cacao liqueur

30 ml Espresso coffee (freshly made & hot)

Hop Toad 1

Resembles an apricot Daiquiri that's heavy on the lime yet balanced.
Ingredientes
30 ml Rum - White/gold 1-3 year old mellow light
30 ml Apricot brandy liqueur
30 ml Lime juice (freshly squeezed)
10 ml Chilled water (omit if using wet ice)

The Boulevardier

Ingredientes
2 ounces rye or bourbon
1 ounces Campari
1 ounce sweet vermouth

Boulevard

A Manhattan-style cocktail which takes no prisoners.
Ingredientes
75 ml Whiskey - Bourbon whiskey

15 ml Grand Marnier liqueur
30 ml Vermouth - Dry
2 Orange bitters

Hollywood Blvd

Mustard is perhaps an unlikely fit with rum,
pineapple and lemon juice but they sit
together in this ...
Ingredientes
50 ml Rum - 6-10yr old Caribbean blended
rum
25 ml Pineapple juice (fresh pressed)
15 ml Lemon juice (freshly squeezed)
15 ml Honey water (1:1)
2.5 ml Dijon Mustard

A.m.f (Adios Mother * Censored*)

This drink is a favorite of mine when I've had
a bad day and just want one good stiff drink
to put ...
Ingredientes
3/4 ounce vodka
3/4 ounce gin

3/4 ounce light rum
3/4 ounce tequila
3/4 ounce blue curacao

Jack Frost

Spicy and fruity, with whiskey dominating the flavor.

Ingredientes
45 ml Whiskey - Tennessee whiskey
15 ml Drambuie liqueur
22.5 ml Suco fresco de Laranja
15 ml Suco fresco de Limão Siciliano
7.5 ml Grenadine/pomegranate syrup

Galliano hot shot

Glass type
Shot glass
3 ingredients
2 cl Galliano
2 cl Whipped Cream
2 cl Coffee

Cozonac

Glass type
Shot glass
3 ingredients
1/3 part Baileys Irish Cream
1/3 part Jagermeister
1/3 part Stroh Rum (80% Alcohol)
Mississippi Gambler
Glass type
Shot glass
4 ingredients
¼ Kahlua
¼ Southern Comfort
¼ Creme De Menthe
¼ Bols Blue Curacao

Darjeeling Insignia

Glass type
Shot glass
3 ingredients
1 part Kahlua
1 part Creme De Menthe
1 part Amarula Cream

Flaming Bob Marley Shot
4 ingredientes
1 part Grenadine
1/2 part 151 proof rum
1/2 part Creme de menthe, Green
1 part Galliano

Noble-Rita

Ingredients
2 oz Casa Noble Crystal Tequila
1 oz agave nectar
1 oz lime juice
Lime wedge

Preparation
Place ingredients, except lime wedge, into a shaker with ice.
Shake until chilled.
Strain into glass (salt rim optional).
Garnish with lime wedge.

Noble Paloma

Ingredients
2 oz Casa Noble Crystal Tequila
1 oz lime juice
1 oz grapefruit juice
0.5 oz agave nectar
Sparkling water
Grapefruit wedge

Buried Treasure

Ingredients
2 oz Casa Noble Crystal Tequila
0.75 oz orange-chamomile simple syrup
0.5 oz lemon juice
0.25 oz spiced rum
2 dashes bitters
Orange zest
Tarragon sprig

Spicy Buck

Ingredients
2 oz Casa Noble Reposado Tequila
2 thin slices jalapeño
1 Tbsp sliced ginger
1 oz lemon juice
0.75 oz simple syrup
Ginger ale or ginger beer
Dash bitters
Lemon wedge

Noble Twist

Ingredients
1.5 oz Casa Noble Añejo Tequila
0.5 oz lemon juice
0.5 oz lime juice
0.25 oz green chartreuse
0.5 oz simple syrup
Lemon peel

Preparation
Place all ingredients, except lemon peel, in glass; add ice and swizzle.

Squeeze lemon peel; rub around rim and drop into glass.

Sazerac
Ingredients:
1 tsp Ricard
1/2 tsp superfine Sugar
2 dashes Peychaud bitters
1 tsp Water
2 oz Bourbon
1 twist of Lemon peel

Aperol Gin Sour

Ingredients
45 mL Aperol
45 mL London Dry Gin
25 mL Lemon Juice
1 Egg White
1 tsp Agave Syrup

Preparation
Dry shake the egg white to emulsify
Add ice and the remaining ingredients to a cocktail shaker

Shake & double strain into a cocktail glass

Yellow Bird

Ingredients
1.5 cl Galliano
1.5 cl Lime Juice
1.5 cl Triple Sec
3 cl White Rum

Absinthe Cocktail

Ingredients
45 ml (1 1/2 oz.) anise liqueur (like Absinthe)
15 ml (1/2 oz.) orange juice
2 drops angostura
Ice cubes
1 star anise

Orange Blue Le Bou

Ingredients
50 ml whiskey
100 ml of orange juice
15 ml blue curacao

3 ice stones

Preparation
In a glass or drink glass add one ingredient at a
time. Serve immediately

Saratoga Cocktail

- ¾oz Brandy,
- 2dash Angostura Bitter,
- ¾oz Sweet Vermouth,
- ¾oz Rye Whiskey

A unique cocktail using 3 kinds of base spirits.
To great success I think! Stir with ice, before
straining into a cold glass.

Jack Rose Cocktail

- ¾ shots lemon juice,
- ¼ shots Sugar Syrup,
- 2 dashes Angostura Bitter,
- 2 shots Calvados,
- ¼ shots Pomegranate Syrup

This well balanced drink can be enhanced
with the addition of an egg white prior to

shaking. Pour all ingredients into a shaker with ice, shake well then strain into chilled cocktail glass.

Raspberry Limoncello Prosecco

• 6x mint Leaves,
• 1cups Limoncello,
• 1cups Raspberry,
• 3cups Prosecco

Simple to make, fresh tangy ingredients, combine to make a delicious cocktail. Simple mix together the Prosecco and limoncello in a pitcher with ice. In each glass that you are serving to, add some frozen raspberries before dropping in a sprig of fresh mint. Simple, yet tasty,

Ritz

Orange undertones to the decadent champagne make this one a winner all round.
7.5ml Cointreau
22.5ml Orange Juice
22.5ml Cognac

120ml Champagne

Comte de Sureau

A gin, campari, whisky combination. Watch
out for this one, it's got quite the kick!
4 cl Gin
1 cl Campari
3 cl Whiskey

Strawberry Margarita

• 1 oz Lime Juice,
• 1 oz Triple Sec,
• 1 1/2 oz Tequila,
• 1 1/2 oz Strawberry Schnapps
Shake all ingredients in a cocktail shaker with
ice. shake well for 10-15 seconds or until the
outside of the shaker becomes frosted. Strain
into cocktail glass.

Spring on 1st Avenue

• ½ oz Grand Marnier,
• 1 oz Lime Juice,

- 1 ½ oz Tequila Blanco,
- 2 oz Beetroot Juice,
- ½ oz mint Syrup

Invented by Evelyn Chick of Vancouver. Pour all ingredients into a shaker with ice. shake well then strain into a highball glass with crushed ice. Garnish with a mint sprig.

Sweet Dream

- 0.5 cl Lime Juice,
- 4.5 cl Bombay Sapphire Gin,
- 0.5 cl Martini Dry,
- 1.5 cl Créme de Pomme,
- 0.5 cl Marie Brizard Grand Orange

Devised by Walter Rolando Davaldos Cardenas from Peru, this cocktail not only won the Before Dinner Cocktail but also the overall 2012 Champion of Champions Cocktail at the IBA Cocktail Competition in 2012, Pour all ingredients into a mixing glass with ice. Stir well to combine.

Newcastle Skittles

- 1 shot Vodka,
- Lemonade,
- Orange,
- 1 shot Blue Taboo,
- 1 shot Bols Blue Curacao

Add 1 shot of Blue Curacao, 1 shot of Blue Taboo, and 1 Shot of vodka to a glass then fill up with equal measures of orange and lemonade. The original Newcastle recipe for the skittles cocktail.

Dorchester

- 0.75oz Lime Juice,
- 0.5oz Sugar Syrup,
- 0.5oz Grapefruit Juice,
- 1.5oz London Dry Gin,
- 0.25oz Maraschino cherry liqueur

Featured on Common Man Cocktails Add all ingredients to a shaker filled with ice.
Shake for 10-15 second.
Double strain into chilled cocktail glass.
Garnish with a grapefruit twist.

Chambord Margarita Royale

- 1/2 oz Lime Juice,
- 3/2 oz Chambord,
- 3/2 oz Pomegranate Juice,
- 1 1/2 oz Tequila Silver

Shake all ingredients in a cocktail shaker with ice. shake well for 10-15 seconds or until the outside of the shaker becomes frosted. Strain into cocktail glass.

Berentzen Peppermint Patty

- 1 oz Chocolate Liqueur,
- 0.75 oz Berentzen Icemint

Pour all ingredients into a shaker with ice. shake well then strain into rocks filled lowball glass. Garnish with a sprig of mint and serve.

Southern Style Julep Cocktail
- 8 mint Leaves,
- Dash Sugar,
- 1 oz Jamaican Rum,
- 2 oz Bourbon

In a mixing glass muddle the sugar with the mint leaves and a dash of the bourbon. Add the rest of the bourbon and Jamaican Rum, before shaking with ice and straining a crushed ice filled lowball glass.

Rob Roy

- Dash Angostura Bitter,
- 30 ml Sweet Vermouth,
- 1 ½ oz Scotch Whisky

Add all the ingredients into a mixing glass with ice and stir quite vigorously to combine the ingredients. Strain into a cocktail glass.

Glogg

- 0.2oz Ginger,
- 3oz Sugar,
- 750ml Red Wine,
- 1 Cinnamon,
- 15 Cloves,
- 6 Cardamom pods

A traditional Swedish take on Mulled Wine. Simply add the red wine, sugar, ginger, cinnamon stick, cloves and cardamom into a suitable large saucepan and heat slowly until the flavours have all infused. Do not let the mixture boil. Ladle into quirky Christmas mugs or milk glasses, garnish.

Italian Surfer with a Russian Attitude

- 1 oz Malibu rum,
- 4 oz Pineapple juice,
- Dash Cranberry Juice,
- 1 oz Amaretto,
- 1 oz Russian Standard Vodka

Add all the ingredients into a highball glass with ice. Stir and serve.

Mermaid Mule

- 2oz Vodka,
- 1oz Lime Juice,
- .5oz Ginger Beer,
- 1oz Blue Curacao

What makes these cocktails blue? It's Curaçao, a blue liqueur made from citrus peels! Its tangy flavor is the perfect compliment to your average Moscow Mule. Divide vodka, blue curaçao, and lime juice between 3 glasses and stir to combine. Fill glasses with ice and top off each drink.

Violet Martini

• 1 ½ oz Vanilla Vodka,
• ½ oz Violet Syrup
Now typically the Martini is a Gin drink. Although Vodka comes as a very trendy and fit replacement, it still counts as some kind of surrogate. And despite all that I just can imagine a Gin variant of the Violet Martini - the vanilla adds its unique aroma, and hence we have this cocktail.

Violet Daiquiri

• 1 oz Lime Juice,
• 2 oz White Rum,
• 1 tbsp Violet Syrup
I mixed this and while enjoying it I found that it was already blogged about. The Monins Violet syrup's unique taste and aroma actually

makes your imagination to be daring and go wild. Yet you still have the urge to revisit some classics through its lens. It's no surprise that many people.

The St. Hendricks

- .25oz Lime Juice,
- 6 mint Leaves,
- 1 wedge Lime,
- 1.25oz Hendricks Gin,
- 3-4oz Tonic Water,
- 1 slice Cucumber,
- .5oz Elderflower Liqueur

This refreshing cocktail was created on a hot summer day, as far as I know, up in Traverse city, Michigan @ The Parlor. The following ingredients compliment each other very well. Muddle the cucumber, mint, and lime wedge in a pint glass.

She's a Peach Cocktail

- 15 ml lemon juice,
- 45 ml Black Rum,

- 15 ml Peach Nectar,
- 15 ml Ginger Syrup

Created by Danielle Tatarin of The Designer Cocktail Company, and featured in BC Liquor Taste magazine under an article for signature wedding cocktails. Combine the peach nectar, lemon juice and ginger syrup in a cocktail tin, before adding the black rum and ice. shake well and strain.

King Louis Cocktail

- 10ml White Rum,
- 10ml Banana Liqueur,
- 10ml Chocolate Liqueur

Never doubt a cocktail that puts the classic banana and chocolate combo together. This one doesn disappoint. Shake up the three ingredients together in a cocktail shaker with ice. Strain into a shot glass and you are away.

Vodka Collins Cocktail

- 1 oz lemon juice,
- Top up with Soda Water,

- 1/2 oz Sugar Syrup,
- 2 oz Ketel One Vodka

Pour all ingredients except the soda water into a shaker with ice. shake well then strain into rocks filled highball glass. Top up with soda water as appropriate.

Chris Cocktail

- ½oz Cointreau,
- ½oz Creme De Cacao,
- 6oz Coffee,
- ¾oz Irish Whiskey

As a fan of specialty coffees, I wanted to make the Irish coffee a little more festive. Adding a few extra touches like a little holiday chocolate orange flavour. Prepare your favourite coffee and add milk sugar to taste. Add the rest of the ingredients and stir. Top with whipped cream if desired.

Captain Jack Sparrow Cocktail

- 2 parts Coke,
- 1 oz Jack Daniels,

• 1 oz Captain Morgans Spiced Rum
Captain (Morgans Spiced Rum) Jack
(Daniels) Sparrow is how the drink got its
name. And it seemed appropriate considering
one or two of these drinks will have you
feeling good. Pour 1 OZ Jack Daniels and 1
OZ Captain Morgan's Spiced Rum into a
lowball glass. Add three ice cubes and top.

Clover Club Cocktail

• 1/4 oz lemon juice,
• 1/4 oz Sugar Syrup,
• 5 fresh Raspberry,
• 1 3/2 oz Dry Gin,
• 1/4 oz Sweet Red Vermouth,
• 1/4 oz Dry Vermouth,
• 1/2 Egg white
Pour all ingredients into a shaker with ice.
shake well then strain into chilled cocktail
glass.

Rapunzel Cocktail

• 1.5oz Ginger Ale,

• 1oz St Germain Elderflower Liqueur,
• 1oz Pear vodka

Created by Joshua Zollo, this drink is based on the Lily of the Sun by Cody. Fill a short rocks glass with ice

Add 1 oz St. Germain Elderflower Liqueur

Add 1 oz Pear Vodka

Top with 1.5 oz ginger ale.

Berentzen Pear Sidecar Cocktail
• Splash lemon juice,
• 1 oz Cognac,
• ½ oz Berentzen Pear

Pour all ingredients into a shaker with ice. shake well then strain into chilled cocktail glass. Garnish with a lemon twist and serve.

Copacabana Cocktail
• 3/2 oz Cream,
• 3/2 oz apple juice,
• 1 3/2 oz Cachaca,
• 3/2 oz Chocolate Syrup,
• 1 1/2 oz Papaya juice

Shake all ingredients in a cocktail shaker with ice. shake well for 10-15 seconds or until the outside of the shaker becomes frosted. Strain into highball glass with crushed ice.

Madeleine Cocktail

- 12 cl Pineapple juice,
- 1 cl Gin,
- 2 cl Passoa,
- 1 cl Coconut liqueur

Aromatic and delicious passion fruit themed tropical drink. It is centred around Passoa, but I guess any Passion Fruit liqueur can be used instead. Pour all ingredients into a shaker with ice. shake well then strain into chilled hurricane glass (the classic cocktail glass also can be used).

Canadian Club Sweet Old Fashioned Cocktail

- 2 shots Canadian Club Whisky,
- 2 slices Orange,
- 1 shots Sugar Syrup,
- 1 dash Angostura Bitter,
- 2 ml Maraschino Cherry

This is a twist on the traditional old fashioned Take 1 slice of orange and 1 Maraschino cherry in a large glass or tumbler with ice. Add 1 dash of Angostura bitters and 1 dash of Peychaud's bitters.

Lemon Cheesecake Cocktail

- Pinch of zest from a Lemon,
- 35 ml Vanilla Vodka,
- 1 tbsp Vanilla Syrup,
- 1 tbsp Natural Yoghurt,
- 1 tbsp Mascarpone

Invented by Wayne Collins and premiered on Something for the Weekend, this cheesecake inspired cocktail makes a perfect after dinner treat. Place all the ingredients into a cocktail shaker with ice, and shake hard. Strain into a cocktail glass and garnish with some digestive biscuit on.

Smoked Pear Cocktail

- 1 ½ oz Gin,
- ¼ oz Raspberry Liqueur,

- ¾ oz Pear Liqueur,
- ¼ oz Mezcal,
- ¾ oz Lillet Blanc

Add all the ingredients into a cocktail glass with ice. Stir for around 20 seconds to mix the ingredients fully. Strain into a cocktail glass and garnish with a flaming orange twist.

Berentzen Apple Sour Cocktail

- 1.25 oz Vodka,
- 1 oz lemon juice,
- 1 oz Soda Water,
- 1.25 oz Berentzen Apple

Add all the ingredients to a tall glass over ice. Stir before garnishing with a lemon slice.

Hurricane Cocktail

- 1/2 oz Lime Juice,
- 1 oz Pineapple juice,
- 1 oz orange juice,
- 1 1/2 oz White Rum,
- 3/2 oz Lime Cordial,
- 1 oz Gold Rum,

• 1/4 oz Passionfruit Syrup
Pour all ingredients into a shaker with ice.
shake well then strain into chilled cocktail
glass.

Apple-Pom Mocktini Cocktail

• 2 oz orange juice,
• Splash Pomegranate Juice,
• 2 oz Non-alcoholic Apple Cider
Pour the apple cider and __orange juice into a
cocktail __shaker with ice. Shake and strain
into a martini glass. Top up with a splash of
the pomegranate juice, before garnishing with
an apple slice and cinnamon stick.

New Port Codebreaker Cocktail

• 120ml orange juice,
• 15ml Advocaat,
• 15ml Coconut Cream,
• 30ml Tequila Reposado,
• 30ml Overproof Rum
An unusual yet surprisingly effective
combination of ingredients. Shake all the

ingredients in a cocktail shaker with ice. Strain into an ice filled highball glass and serve.

Spice 75 Cocktail

• 18ml Lime Juice,
• 40ml Rum,
• 12ml Sugar Syrup,
• 120ml Champagne,
• Dash Allspice

A nice winter spiced take on the classic French 75. Shake all the ingredients except the champagne in a cocktail __shaker with ice. Strain into a champagne flute before topping up with champagne. Garnish with an orange twist and serve - delicious.

Fog Cutter Cocktail

• 45 ml __orange juice,
• 45 ml Bacardi Superior Rum,
• 15 ml __lemon juice,
• 12.5 ml Cognac,
• 15 ml Sherry Sweet,
• 15 ml Dry Gin,

• 15 ml Orgeat Syrup

Shake all the ingredients, except the sherry, with ice and strain into ice-filled highball glass. Float the sherry on top of the drink, garnish with an orange wheel and serve.

Alaska Ice Tea Cocktail

• 20 ml Vodka,
• 20 ml Cointreau,
• 20 ml White Rum,
• 20 ml Gin,
• 20 ml Bols Blue Curacao

Build in a highball glass. Fill with Sprite/7up. Decorate with a lime wedge.

Norwegian Wood Cocktail

• 3/2 oz Sweet Vermouth,
• 1 oz Aquavit,
• 1 oz Apple Brandy,
• 1/4 oz Yellow Chartreuse

Created by Jeffrey Morgenthaler of Clyde Commons in Portland when he was challenged to make something with aquavit.

Add all the ingredients into a mixing glass with ice and stir. Strain into a chilled cocktail glass.

Malibu Seabreeze Cocktail

• 1par Malibu rum,
• 1part Pineapple juice,
• 1part Cranberry Juice

Fill your highball glass with crushed ice. Add equal parts of Malibu Rum, Cranberry Juice and Pine__apple juice. Optional: Add a lime wedge and a sprig of__ mint.

The BEMCo Cocktail

• 2oz Vodka,
• 1oz Lime Juice,
• 4oz Coke,
• 1/4oz Sugar Syrup

Delicious. You will not taste the Alcohol. Developed at Brandeis University. Shake all the ingredients except the coke with ice. Strain into an ice-filled rocks glass. Top with Coke, and garnish with a lime wedge.

Coronation Cocktail Cocktail

- 1 dash Apricot Brandy,
- 0.75 oz Sweet Vermouth,
- 0.75 oz Apple Brandy,
- 0.75 oz Dry Vermouth

Add all the ingredients into a mixing glass with ice. Stir before straining into a chilled cocktail glass.

Old Fashioned Cocktail

- 12.5 ml Sugar Syrup,
- 3 dashes Angostura Bitter,
- 60 ml Bourbon

Muddle the sugar with the Angostura bitter and soda water in a lowball glass. Fill the glass with ice and add the bourbon. The Old Fashioned can be served with bourbon or normal whiskey.

Fancy Free Cocktail

- 1dash Orange Bitters,

- 1dash Angostura Bitter,
- 2oz Bourbon,
- 0.5oz Maraschino cherry liqueur

Stir all the ingredients with ice and then strain into a cocktail glass.

Greyhound Cocktail

- 5 cl Vodka,
- 15 cl Grapefruit Juice

A simple classic, just add the ingredients with ice to a highball glass, stir and enjoy.

Mudslide Cocktail

- 5 cl Baileys Irish Cream,
- 2.5 cl Tia Maria,
- Top up Chocolate Milk,
- Top up Double Cream

Shake the baileys and tia Maria in a cocktail __shaker with ice. Strain into a lowball glass and add the desired amount of chocolate milk. Finally add some squirty cream on top.

Berentzen Apple Sour Cocktail

- 1.25 oz Vodka,
- 1 oz lemon juice,
- 1 oz Soda Water,
- 1.25 oz Berentzen Apple

Add all the ingredients to a tall glass over ice. Stir before garnishing with a lemon slice.

Happy V-Day

Ingredients
1.5 oz vodka
.75 oz blood orange liqueur
1.5 oz orange juice
1 splash lemon juice
5 chopped berries (raspberries and strawberries)
1 tsp sugar or 1/2 packet of sweetener
1/2 can lemon-lime soda like Sprite
1 sprinkle chocolate shavings for garnish
Instructions
Combine vodka, liqueur, orange juice, lemon juice and sugar /sweetener and shake vigorously.

Wet and dip glass rim in pink or red sugar crystals.

Fill glass with ice cubes.

Pour shaken mixture over ice. Add sprite and stir to mix.

Sprinkle with chocolate shavings.

Santa's Whiskey Flip

Ingredients

2 ounces cinnamon-infused bourbon whiskey

1/2 ounce amaretto

1 whole egg

Optional: 2 teaspoons heavy cream

Garnish: grated nutmeg

1. In a cocktail shaker, combine the whiskey, amaretto, and egg. Add cream if you like.

2. Dry shake (without ice) vigorously.

3. Fill the shaker with ice and shake again for 30 seconds.

4. Strain into a chilled sour or cocktail glass.

5. Dust with grated nutmeg.

Make your own Cinnamon Infused Whisky:

To make cinnamon whiskey, simply place two whole cinnamon sticks into a mason jar filled with bourbon. Shake well and store in a cool, dark place for about three days, shaking it daily. After the third day, give your infusion a taste test.

Chamomile Honey Syrup Cocktails

Ingredients
3/4 water
1/3 cup honey
1-2 chamomile tea bags

3 ounces fresh grapefruit juice (about half of 1 grapefruit
2-4 tablespoons chamomile honey syrup depending on your taste
2 ounces tequila omit to make a virgin version
4 fresh strawberries sliced
sparkling water for topping off
crushed ice

* Combine water and honey in a small saucepan and bring to a low boil, simmer for 1 minute and remove from the heat.

* Add the tea bag, cover and steep for 5-10 minutes.
* Remove the tea bag and allow the syrup to cool completely.
*Store in the fridge.

The drink
*Add the grapefruit juice, chamomile syrup, tequila and strawberries to a glass.
* Use a muddler (or even the end of a rolling pin), gently push the strawberries down until they release their juices and are slightly smashed.
* Add a handful of ice and then add sparkling water to top off.
* Give the drink a gentle stir.
* Taste and add more chamomile syrup if desired. Garnish with fresh chamomile flowers and strawberries if desired.

NYE Rose Cocktail

Ingrediets
2-3 scoops raspberry sorbet
1 cup rose champagne

fresh raspberries for garnish

Place scoops of sorbet in a large wine glass.
Pour champagne over the sorbet.
Top with raspberries.
Allow to melt while you sip or eat with a
spoon.

Christmas Jingle Juice

Ingredients
4 c. Cran-Apple Juice
2 bottles red moscato
1 bottle prosecco
1/2 c. vodka
2 c. frozen cranberries
1/3 c. mint leaves
1/2 c. sugar, for rimming glasses
2 limes, sliced into rounds

Using a wedge of lime, wet the rim of your
glasses. Dip in sugar until coated.
Combine all ingredients in a punch bowl, stir
together and serve.

Long Island Apple Iced Tea

Ingredients
1 oz triple sec
1 oz white rum
1 oz gin
1 oz apple vodka
4 oz apple cider
2 oz lemon-lime soda

Instructions
Add triple sec, white rum, gin, vodka, and apple cider to shaker. Shake for 20-30 seconds to combine.
Strain equally into 2 glasses filled with ice.
Top each with 1 oz lemon-lime soda.
Garnish with apple slices, if desired, and straw.

Witches Brew

Ingredients
2 1/2 oz Midori melon liqueur
2 1/2 oz lemon-lime soda (sprite)
2 1/2 oz orange juice

Add ice to a cocktail shaker and pour ingredients in. Cover and shake until chilled, then pour into martini glasses and serve.
Notes:
Add black sanding sugar to a small plate, rim the glass with a wedge of lemon or lime. Dip the rim of the martini into sanding sugar.

Add a pinch of edible luster dust for a subtle sheen.
Reduce lemon-lime soda to 1 1/2 oz, and add 1 oz vodka for a stronger drink.
To make non-alcoholic, use 3 1/2 oz orange juice and 4 oz lemon-lime soda, then add a few drops of green food coloring.

The fall

Ingredients:
2.5 parts BACARDÍ Reserva Ocho
2.5 parts Sugar syrup
1 part Freshly-pressed apple juice
2 dashes Orange Bitters
Directions:

Build over rocks until perfectly diluted. Float apple juice last. Garnish with an apple fan.

Easy and delicious

Ingredients:
2 ounces Jamaican Rum (Appleton)
1/4 cup Pineapple Juice
1/4 cup Mango Juice
2 tablespoons Lime Juice
1 tablespoon Grenadine
Directions:
Stir all ingredients together well. Pour over ice. Garnish with pineapple slices and lime slices.

Pimm's Cup

A palmful of mint leaves
2 fingers' worth of cucumber (about two 1/2-inch thick slices)
1 large or 2 medium strawberries
2 ounces Pimm's No. 1
1 large squeeze of lemon
Best quality ginger ale

1. Add the mint, cucumber slices, and strawberry to the bottom of the shaker, and muddle with a muddler or the handle of a sturdy wooden spoon. Pour in the Pimm's No. 1, then the squeeze of lemon. Fill the shaker with ice, and shake for a good ten seconds.

2. Double strain into a Collins glass filled with ice, and top with ginger ale. Garnish with a cucumber slice and a sprig of mint.

Watermelon and Tequila

Ingredients
1/4 cup water
1/4 cup granulated sugar
8 cups diced seedless watermelon (1 pound)
1/4 cup fresh lime juice
1 3/4 cups blueberries
3/4 cup lightly packed fresh mint leaves, plus 8 sprigs for garnish
1 1/4 cups silver tequila Ice

How to Make It

Step 1   (Or you can use store bought simple syrup)

In a small saucepan, bring the water to a simmer with the sugar and stir over moderate heat until the sugar is dissolved, about 1 minute; let the sugar syrup cool.

Step 2

In a blender, puree the watermelon until smooth. Set a fine-mesh strainer over a bowl and strain the watermelon juice, pressing gently on the solids to extract as much juice as possible. Discard the pulp.

Step 3

In a large pitcher, combine the sugar syrup with the lime juice, blueberries and mint leaves. Using a wooden spoon, lightly muddle the blueberries and mint. Add the watermelon juice and tequila. Refrigerate until chilled, about 2 hours.

Step 4

Pour the cocktail into tall ice-filled glasses. Garnish with the mint sprigs and serve.

Blue Crush Margarita

- Start with a frosted glass.
- Fill with Ice.
- Slide a lime slice around the edge of the glass and dip the glass in salt.
- Fill the glass with Ice.
- Pour 1 part, blue curacao.
- Pour 1/2 part lime juice.
- Pour 2 parts Tequila.
- Pour 1/2 part Triple Sec.
- Top with Club Soda and garnish with a lime.

Bourbini

Ingredients
1 oz. Heaven Hill 6-year bourbon
2 dashes peach bitters
.5 oz. Mathilde Peche peach liqueur
Sparkling wine
Shake ingredients with ice, strain into flute, top with sparkling wine, and garnish with mint sprig.

Celebrating with friends and family

Ingredients
For the chocolate Guinness jello shot portion:
1/2 cup cold Guinness Stout
2 envelopes unflavored gelatin
1/4 cup Patron Cafe
1/4 cup Creme de Cacao or just 1/2 cup
Creme de Cacao if not using Patron
1 cup hot water
For the Bailey's jello shot portion:
1/2 cup Bailey's Irish Cream
1 envelope unflavored gelatin
1/2 cup hot water

Instructions
For the chocolate Guinness jello shot portion:
Add Guinness to a medium bowl, sprinkle on
both envelopes of gelatin, and allow to sit for
one minute.
Stir in Patron, creme de cacao and hot water
until the gelatin is completely dissolved.
Evenly divide the chocolate Guinness jello
shot mixture into individual shot glass cups

and refrigerate immediately for 15-20 minutes. NOTE: Mine made exactly 15.
For the Bailey's jello shot portion:
Once the Guinness portion has chilled, add the Bailey's Irish Cream to a medium bowl, sprinkle on the packet of gelatin, and allow to sit for one minute.

Pour hot water into the Bailey's jello shot mixture and stir until the gelatin is completely dissolved.

Gently pour the Bailey's jello shot mixture over the chilled Guinness mixture.

Refrigerate for 3 hours or until completely set.

St. Patrick's Day

6 scoops vanilla ice cream
2 c. Guinness
1/2 c. Baileys
1/4 c. hot fudge
Directions
Scoop three scoops ice cream each into two tall glasses. Pour 1 cup Guinness and 1/4 cup

Baileys over each serving. Drizzle with hot fudge.
Serve immediately.

Passion Fruit Caipiroska

2 oz passion fruit juice
1 oz simple syrup, 1:1 ratio, cooled
2 oz Tito's Handmade Vodka
1 oz lime juice
1/2 oz lemon juice
Edible flower for garnish

Preparation:
In a cocktail shaker filled with ice, combine all ingredients. Shake vigorously and strain into a stemmed glass. Garnish with an edible flower.

Strawberry Skyy Cocktail

Ingredients:
2 oz Wild strawberry Skyy vodka or other strawberry infused vodka
2 oz White creme de cacao
5 oz strawberries about 1 cup, fresh or frozen

1 cup ice
3 oz of vanilla ice cream 2 full scoops
For decoration:
2 oz chocolate of choice for decoration
fresh strawberries for decoration

Chocolate Ganache for Dipping the Glasses:
Pour about an inch of water in a small pot,
and bring to a gentle simmer.
Chop the chocolate into equal pieces, and
place in a heat-safe bowl (and one, that is flat
bottomed and wide enough to enclose the rim
of the glasses) over the simmering water, so
that the bowl does not come in direct contact
with the water.
Stir constantly, until about 80% of the
chocolate has melted. Remove from the heat,
and stir until all the chocolate is melted.
Dip the glasses in the melted chocolate. You
can tilt them slightly to create the wavy effect,
then turn upside down, and allow the
chocolate to drip on the sides slightly.
The Cocktail

Place all ingredients (except the solid chocolate) in a blender, and process until smooth.
Pour the cocktail in the prepared glasses and garnish with a fresh strawberry.

Dreaming of You

Ingredients:
4 oz Moscato
1.5 oz Pomegranate Juice
1 oz Pink grapefruit juice
Splash Soda water
Directions: Build in glass over ice and stir.

Heart-shaped candies cocktails

Recipe:
1.5 oz Encanto Pisco
.75 oz Pineau des Charentes
.5 oz Small Hand Foods pineapple syrup
.25 oz one of the following: Framboise (pink), Mandarine Napoleon (orange), blue curaçao (blue)
.75 oz lime juice

.75 oz egg white
.75 oz sparkling wine
Directions:
Combine all ingredients except sparkling wine
in a shaker without ice. Shake, then add ice
and shake again. Strain into a large cocktail
glass. Add sparkling wine.
For Garnish: Cut a stencil out of a sturdy
plastic sheet and spray over a cocktail with
Angostura bitters.

Mocktail or Cocktail

1 kiwi
3 teaspoons pineapple juice
1 teaspoon (or more if you like it sweet) raw
honey
1 can La Croix sparkling lemon water
*optional: ice cubes with fresh mint leaves
For the real thing substitute the La Croix with
a little Prosecco and freshly squeezed lemon
juice.
Instructions
1. Peel and slice the kiwi and place into a
small food processor or blender

2. Add the pineapple juice and raw honey (honey should be warmed a few seconds in the microwave so it is in a liquid state)
3. Pulse or blend to make a thin, well-blended puree
4. Pour 3/4 cup sparkling water into each glass.
5. Divide the puree and pour into each glass Serve with mint ice cubes if desired.

Pick me up

Ingredients:
1 1/2 ounces chocolate liqueur (Dorda Double Chocolate Liqueur)
1 ounce (or 3 depending on your day) espresso
1/2 ounce amaretto liqueur
For Garnish:
Cappuccino milk foam and/or whipped cream.

Winter Sangria

Ingredients:

1 bottle of sweet red wine
1 bottle sparkling cran-apple cider
2 clementines, sliced thin, peel on
2 granny smith apples, cored and diced
1/2 cup pomegranate arils
1 cup cranberries sliced in half
Rosemary to garnish each glass
Directions:
Mix wine, cider, and fruit in a large pitcher.
Serve over ice and garnish with rosemary.

North Pole
Who's ready for the best tasting North Pole
Cocktail in a glass?
4 ounces vodka
2 ounces Kahlúa or more to taste
4 tablespoons chocolate syrup
1 teaspoon vanilla extract
3 teaspoons molasses
1/8 teaspoon ginger
1/2 cup heavy cream or whole milk
whipped cream candy canes and gingerbread
cookies, for serving (optional)
In a cocktail shaker combine the vodka,
Kahlúa, chocolate syrup, vanilla, molasses,

and ginger. Shake until well combined. Add ice and shake again. Strain into 4 glasses. Top off each glass with heavy cream. Dollop with whipped cream and garnish as desired.

Mama Left Bahama

Enjoy this mouthwatering cocktail relaxing by the sand
Courtesy of Sebastian Krause, TGI Friday's
Bergen - Norway
1 1/4 oz. Bacardi Mango
1 1/4 oz. Cranberry Juice
1/4 oz. Lemon Juice
1/4 oz. Lime Juice
1/2 oz. Monin Agave Syrup
1/2 Passion Fruit seeds
1 Banana Slice (aprox. 1 cm. wide)
Muddle one slice of banana
Pour all the liquids to the mixing tin, add seeds of half passion fruit.
Shake it with ice and strain loosely over the ice in balloon glass with ice cubes.
Garnish with pineapple leaf and half passion fruit.

Bourbon Spiked Hot Apple Cider

Ingredients
4 cups apple cider
1 cinnamon stick
1 tablespoon orange juice
3 whole cloves
1 star anise
Bourbon (recommend Bulleit or Basil Hayden's)
To make the hot cider:
Place the apple cider, cinnamon stick, orange juice, cloves and star anise in a small pot and bring to a boil. Lower to a simmer for 5-10 minutes. Remove from heat and strain into a pitcher.
To make the drink:
In the glass add 2 oz bourbon and 1 cup of the cider mix.
Garnish with an orange slice and stick of cinnamon.

Swamp Monster

Easy peasy last-minute punch.

Serves 18 to 20
1/2 gallon lime sherbet
3 cups vodka, chilled
1 (46-ounce) can unsweetened pineapple
juice, chilled
1-liter ginger ale, chilled
1-liter lemon-lime soda, chilled
Matcha green tea powder, for garnish
(optional)
Place the sherbet in a punch bowl. Pour in the
vodka, pineapple juice, ginger ale, and lemon-
lime soda. Stir well. Rim the edge of each glass
with green tea powder and serve immediately.
A little tang

Ingredients
16 ounces limoncello (lemon-flavored
liqueur)
12 ounces gin
8 ounces fresh lemon juice
24 paper–thin lemon slices Ice

16 ounces chilled club soda
 8 mint sprigs
Instructions
In a pitcher, combine the limoncello, gin and lemon juice. Cover and refrigerate until chilled, at least 2 hours.
Press 3 thin lemon slices against the inside of each of 8 collins glasses.
Add ice to the glasses.
Stir the limoncello mixture and pour it into the glasses.
Stir 2 ounces of club soda into each drink and garnish with a mint sprig.

Eclipse 2017

Ingredients
1.5 oz Patrón XO Cafe
.75 oz Fresh lemon juice
.5 oz Simple syrup
4 oz Aranciata (Italian orange) soda
Half slice blood or Valencia orange for garnish

Fill a highball glass with ice and add all liquid ingredients in order. Garnish with half a slice of blood orange or Valencia orange.

Grilled Peaches

Ingredients
Roasted Peach Old Fashioned cocktail combines caramelized roasted peaches, orange bitters, and bourbon whiskey to make a classic drink even better.
Recipe type: cocktail
Serves: 1
Instructions
Place peach slices on a sheet pan and broil for 3-4 minutes until slightly charred and caramelized.
Place 1 roasted peach slice in a rocks glass with orange rind slice, cherry, sugar cube, and bitters. Muddle together.
Pour in bourbon, splash of soda or water, top with ice, and give a quick stir. Garnish glass with additional peach slices.

Tea Sangria with Raspberries and Peaches

Ingredients
6 cups sweet tea
1 bottle white wine
2 cups raspberries
2 cups sliced peaches
fresh mint, for garnishing (optional)

Instructions
Mix sweet tea and wine together in a large
pitcher. Add fruit and chill for at least 2-3
hours, preferably 8 or more.
Serve in pretty glasses and garnish with mint.
Muddle the fruit for a big more flavor if
you're in a hurry.

Pineapple Ginger Prosecco Punch

Ingredients
2 cups frozen pineapple chunks
4 Dorot Chopped Ginger Cubes (are the
easiest route).
4 cups pineapple juice
1/2 cup cilantro, chopped or 2 Dorot
Chopped Cilantro Cubes

1 750 ml bottle Prosecco (substitute lemon-lime soda for mocktail version)
1/2 cup tequila, optional (but better)

Instructions
Add frozen (or fresh) pineapple to the blender.
Add pineapple juice.
Add ginger and cilantro.
Blend until all the pineapple is chopped up.
Remove from the blender and add to the pitcher.
When ready to serve, pour in Prosecco and tequila.
Garnish with fresh cilantro if desired.

Peach Basil Moscow Mule

ingredients
¼ cup fresh basil
1 large lemon (quartered)
8 oz peach vodka
24 oz ginger beer
Instructions

Fill four glasses with ice. Preferably copper cups - they keep the drink COLD, but any cocktail glass will work!

Add 2 oz vodka and 6 oz ginger beer to each glass.

Squeeze one quarter of a lemon into each glass, then add a couple pieces of fresh basil. Stir all of the ingredients together.

Cherry Soda with a Tingle

Ingredients
½ cup fresh cherries, pitted
¼ teaspoon Madagascar Bourbon Pure Vanilla Extract
1.5 oz (one shot) bourbon
3 teaspoons superfine sugar
1 teaspoon lemon juice
ice cubes
club soda (1/4 cup or so)
In the bottom of a glass, combine the cherries, vanilla extract, bourbon, sugar and lemon juice. Muddle together until cherries are broken and juices are released (you can use the

back of a wooden spoon if you don't have a muddler).

Top with ice cubes and a small splash of club soda.

Sangria with Watermelon & Pineapple

Ingredients
1 bottle Moscato wine (750 ml)
1/2 C brandy
1 lime, thinly sliced
2 C watermelon, cubed and cold
2 C Extra Sweet Pineapple, cubed and cold
lemon lime soda, for serving
ice cubes
Pour the wine and brandy into a pitcher and stir to combine. Add the sliced lime, watermelon, and pineapple.
To serve, place some of the fruit in a glass with ice. Pour the sangria over the ice and top with lemon lime soda. Add some of the fruit juice for sweetness.

Relaxing

ingredients
3 ounces tea
2 ounces fresh orange juice
1 ounce bourbon (Bulleit)
2 ounces Jeremiah Weed Sweet Tea Vodka

plum and mango, cut into cubes

Mix tea, orange juice, bourbon and sweet tea vodka in a short glass. Add cubes of fruit and serve with ice. Optional: garnish with fresh mint leaves.

Make a pitcher and let the flavors infuse into the tea for an even tastier cocktail.

Strawberry Pisco Punch

Ingredients:
750 ml bottle of pisco
1 cup St. Germain elderflower liqueur
1 1/2 cups strawberry syrup
1 1/2 cups lime juice
2 750 ml bottles sparkling apple cider
2 limes for garnish
ice block
Strawberry Syrup:
3/4 cup sugar
3/4 cup water
1 1/2 cups strawberries (halved)

Bourbon with a hint of relaxation

Ingredients
2 oz. Reserve bourbon
1 oz. simple syrup
5 mint leaves
1/2 lemon, cut into quarters
Mint sprig, for garnish
Directions: Muddle mint, lemon, and syrup in a mixing glass. Add the bourbon and dry shake. Strain into a double old-fashioned glass over a tea strainer, making sure to squeeze the remaining liquid from the pulp into the glass. Fill with crushed ice and garnish with mint sprig.

More S'mores

Ingredients
1 (3 1/2 ounce) package instant chocolate pudding mix
3/4 cup 2% milk
1/2 cup Fluffed Marshmallow Vodka
8 ounces extra Cool Whip

1/4 cup graham cracker crumbs

1/2 cup Marshmallow Fluff

1 Hershey's Milk Chocolate Bar

1. In a large bowl, whisk together the chocolate pudding mix and milk until thick and smooth. Add in the vodka whisking until the mixture is free of lumps and well-combined. Fold in the Cool Whip and mix until no white streaks are visible. Set Aside.

2. Spoon 1 1/2 teaspoons of graham cracker crumbs into the bottom of each mini cordial glass.

3. Place the pudding mixture into a piping bag fitted with a round tip such as the Wilton 1A or simply snip the corner of a zip top bag. Pipe the pudding mixture using a swirl motion into each glass stopping about 1/2 inch before the rim of glass.

4. Spoon or pipe (I used a medium French tip) the Marshmallow Fluff directly onto the pudding mixture. If desired, use a kitchen torch to carefully brown the Marshmallow Fluff and garnish with a piece of the Hershey's Milk Chocolate Bar.

Apples on a stick

Ingredients
2 ounces Apple Cider
2 ounces Caramel Vodka
1 ounce Butterscotch Schnapps
Sliced fresh apple, caramel, and / or cinnamon
sugar for garnish.
Rim your martini glass with caramel or
cinnamon sugar. To get the cinnamon sugar
to stick to the glass, dip the rim in a little apple
cider, then the cinnamon sugar.
Combine the apple cider, caramel vodka, and
butterscotch schnapps in a cocktail shaker
filled with ice. Shake vigorously.
Pour mixture into the rimmed martini glass
and garnish with a slice of fresh apple.

Berry-Prosecco Ice Cream Floats

Serves 4
-- 1 bottle (750 ml) of dry Prosecco
-- 1 pint vanilla ice cream
-- 1 pint of mixed berries (strawberries,
blueberries, raspberries)

-- 1 tablespoon sugar
Toss the berries and sugar together in a bowl. Let sit for 15 minutes. Divide berries into 4 glasses. Add a scoop of vanilla ice cream to each glass and top off with Prosecco.

Tiramisu

* Mix in a cocktail shaker a splash or so of espresso or coffee extract (if not available try a little Kahlua)
* 1/2 oz. Amaretto
* 1/2 oz. Frangelico
* 1 oz white chocolate liqueur
* 1 oz dark chocolate liqueur
Splash of cream optional.
Garnish with dusted cocoa powder & cinnamon.

The Evening Shade from Savuer

Ingredients
1/2 oz. lime juice
3 slices cucumber
2 oz. peach purée

1 1/2 oz. whiskey
3/4 oz. Domaine de Canton ginger liqueur
1/2 oz. PAMA pomegranate liqueur
2 sprigs mint
Muddle lime juice and cucumber in a cocktail shaker; add peach purée, whiskey, liqueurs, and ice. Shake vigorously and strain into a Collins glass filled with cracked ice; garnish with mint sprig.

Blueberry

Ingredients
1 cup fresh or frozen blueberries (plus more for garnish)
1 tablespoon sugar
½ cup water
1 ginger beer (like Crabbies)
3 oz vodka
1 lime (plus more wedges for garnish)
Instructions
1. Put blueberries, sugar and water in a saucepan and bring to a boil. Lower heat and let simmer for 10 minutes. Strain syrup through a sieve over a bowl and set aside.

2. Fill two glasses (or copper mugs) with ice. Squeeze half a lime in both glasses.

3. Divide beer and vodka between two glasses. Stir.

4. Add half the blueberry syrup to each glass (or desired amount, may want less if you do not want it very sweet). Stir.

5. Garnish with lime wedge and blueberries.

New You

Ingredients

Light and refreshing, this cocktail is a great option for a drink that won't give you headaches after a party.

1 cucumber

2 limes, juice only

1 tbsp raw agave nectar

10 fresh mint leaves

½ cup coconut water

3 oz tequila

Ice cubes, mint leaves and sea salt, to serve

Add cucumbers, lime, mint leaves, agave and coconut water into a blender and pulse to obtain a green juice.

Strain and transfer into a pitcher, add tequila and mix to combine.

Place sea salt onto a dish, moisten the rim of a rocks glass with a lime slice, then dip in salt. Fill the glasses with ice cubes, evenly pour the cocktail, decorate with mint leaves and serve.

Boys and Girls

Ingredients
6 ounces bourbon
3 ounces fresh grapefruit juice
2 ounces sweet vermouth
1⅓ ounces grenadine
Lemon twists (for serving)
Maraschino cherries (for serving)
Combine bourbon, grapefruit juice, vermouth, and grenadine in a cocktail shaker filled with ice and shake vigorously until the outside of the shaker is frosty, about 20 seconds. Strain into ice-filled rocks glasses. Garnish each with a lemon twist and a cherry.

My kind of greens

Ingredients
6 leaves fresh mint
2 slices cucumber
2 oz. vodka, the good kind
3/4 oz. lime juice
1/2 oz. simple syrup
Prosecco
Muddle mint and cucumber. Add vodka, lime juice, and simple syrup and shake. Pour over glass with ice. Top with Prosecco.

Crusoe Hemingway

Ingredients:
1 1/2 oz Crusoe spiced rum
1/2 oz Fruitlab orange liqueur
1/2 oz fresh lime juice
1/4 oz fresh grapefruit juice
Glass Types: (Martini/Coupe)
Instructions:
Shake and strain into coupe
Garnish with flamed orange zest.

Summer is around the corner

Ingredients

1 1/2 ounces of whiskey -- (bourbons are yum -- bulleit rye).

juice of two fresh lemons

club soda

honey simple syrup

sweetened lime juice

In a medium size glass combine the whiskey, juice of two fresh lemons (hand squeezed is best), ice then fill the rest of the glass with club soda. Add honey simple syrup to taste. If you're not a big fan of honey use regular simple syrup. Add a splash of sweetened lime juice and garnish with a fresh lemon.

Ghost in the Graveyard

Ingredients

2 ounces black vodka

2 ounces creme de cacao or coffee-flavored liqueur

1 scoop vanilla ice cream

Pinch of finely grated nutmeg, for garnish

In a glass, combine vodka and creme de cacao, and set aside. Place a scoop of ice cream in a highball glass, and slowly pour vodka mixture over ice cream. Garnish with nutmeg; serve immediately.

Screwed-Up Screwdriver

Ingredients
1/4 cup ice
1/2 cup freshly squeezed tangerine juice
1 1/2 ounces black vodka
1 black licorice twist, for serving
Place ice in a tall glass. Pour juice into glass. Pour vodka over the back of a cocktail spoon into glass so it sits on top of juice and creates a layer of black. Slice 1/4 inch off each end of the licorice, and use as a straw. Serve immediately.

Berry Scary Martini

Ingredients
1 cup ice
1 ounce black vodka
2 ounces cherry juice
Fresh raspberries and blueberries, for garnish

Combine ice, vodka, and cherry juice in a cocktail shaker; shake vigorously. Pour into a martini glass. Thread raspberries and blueberries onto a cocktail skewer, and place in the drink. Serve immediately.

Candy-infused vodka, Halloween Party

To make candy-infused vodka, place 1/2 cup of candy into a glass jar. Pour 1/2 cup of vodka over the candy. Seal jar and let sit for at least 24 hours, shaking occasionally. Strain vodka when ready to use and discard any solids. (For Sour Patch Kids-infused vodka, use only red, yellow and orange candy for optimal color.)

Yields about 3/4 cup for candy corn vodka, 2/3 cup for orange Skittles vodka, 1/2 cup for Sour Patch Kids vodka.

Shrunken Heads in Cider, Halloween Party

- •2 cups lemon juice
- 2 tablespoons coarse salt
- 8 large Granny Smith apples
- 32 whole cloves
- 2 gallons apple cider
- 2 (12-ounce) cans frozen lemonade concentrate, thawed
- 2 cups spiced rum

•Preheat the oven to 250 degrees. Line a baking sheet with parchment paper; set aside. In a medium bowl, mix together lemon juice and salt; set aside.

• Peel apples and cut each in half through the stem; remove seeds and core. Using a sharp paring knife, carve a face, as desired, on the rounded side of each apple half. Place apples in lemon mixture for one minute; transfer to paper towels to drain.

• Place apples, face-side up on a prepared baking sheet and transfer to the oven. Let bake until the apples are dry and begin to brown around the edges, about 90 minutes.

Remove apples from baking sheets and press cloves into the "eye" sockets.
• Combine cider, lemonade, and rum (if using) in a large punchbowl; float shrunken heads on top.

Pumpkin Eater Cocktail

Ingredients
•1 1/2 oz Light Rum
•1 oz Orange Curacao
•1/2 oz Triple Sec
•1 oz Orange Juice
•1/2 oz Cream
Add ice and ingredients into the blender and blend well.

Coconut margarita

Ingredients
1 cup sweetened shredded coconut
1/2 teaspoon salt
1/2 cup freshly squeezed lime juice, plus 2 tablespoons for glasses (about 5 limes)
3/4 cup Coco Lopez or cream of coconut

1/2 cup plus 2 tablespoons tequila

1/4 cup Cointreau or other orange liqueur

Step 1

Preheat the oven to 350 degrees. On a rimmed baking sheet, toss coconut with the salt. Spread on sheet; toast in oven, stirring frequently, until golden brown, 8 to 10 minutes. Let cool, then crush with your hands until crumbly.

Step 2

Pour 2 tablespoons lime juice into a shallow dish. Place coconut mixture in another dish. Dip rims of two cocktail glasses in lime juice, then in coconut mixture, coating well.

Step 3

Combine remaining ingredients with 1 cup ice in a blender; puree until smooth. Divide evenly between prepared glasses, and serve immediately.

LA Times

Ingredients:

1 1/2 ounces bonded AppleJack

1/4 ounce maple syrup (or more as desired, depending on the tartness of your apple juice)

6 ounces hot fresh-pressed apple juice (heated in a tea kettle)

3 slices crab apple for garnish, very thinly sliced

Grated cinnamon for garnish

Cinnamon stick for garnish

Into an 8-ounce glass mug, pour the Apple Jack and maple syrup. Top off with the hot apple cider, and stir gently with a spoon. Garnish with slices of crab apple, freshly grated cinnamon and a cinnamon stick.

Printed in Great Britain
by Amazon

10755185R00098